MasterChef
Amazing
Mains

MasterChef
Amazing
Mains

Contents

Amazing Flavours

Visual Feasts

Sheer Indulgence

Amazing
Flavours

Savoy-wrapped pepper bake with aubergines à la Parmigiana and ratatouille

Sara Danesin Medio @ finalist

Preparation time 35 minutes   **Cooking time** 1 hour 35 minutes   **Serves 6**

Ingredients

For the pepper bakes

1 red pepper, deseeded and finely diced

1 yellow pepper, deseeded and finely diced

1 banana shallot, finely chopped

1 tbsp olive oil

salt and freshly ground black pepper

1 sprig of thyme, leaves only

2 eggs

60g (2oz) Parmesan cheese, finely grated

150ml (5fl oz) double cream

9 large Savoy cabbage, leaves, thick stalks removed

butter, for greasing

For the ratatouille

1 Italian aubergine, diced into 1cm (½ in) cubes

1 garlic clove, crushed

1 tbsp olive oil

75g (2½oz) Taggiasca olives, pitted

small bunch of basil leaves, chopped

For the aubergines

3 Italian aubergines

salt

vegetable oil, for deep frying

1 onion, finely chopped

1 tbsp olive oil

1kg (2¼lb) San Marzano or plum tomatoes, skinned, deseeded, and diced

small bunch of basil, leaves chopped

2 buffalo mozzarella cheeses, sliced

100g (3½oz) Parmesan cheese shavings

For the pesto

85g (3oz) basil leaves, plus extra for garnish

1 garlic clove

4 tbsp pine nuts

8 tbsp extra virgin olive oil

4 tbsp grated Parmesan cheese, plus extra for garnish

pinch of salt

To serve

200g (7oz) tomberrries

small handfuls of micro cress

small handfuls of pea shoots

Method

1 Preheat the oven to 180°C (350°F/Gas 4).
Make the pepper bakes. Sauté the peppers
and shallot in the olive oil for around 30 minutes
until soft, occasionally adding a splash of water if
the mixture becomes too dry. Season to taste and
add the thyme leaves, then leave to cool. Once
the mixture has cooled, blitz until smooth in a
food processor and pass through a fine sieve.

2 Whisk together the eggs, Parmesan cheese,
and cream, then add the pepper purée and
mix well.

3 Blanch the cabbage leaves for 2 minutes
in boiling water, then refresh in iced water.
Pat dry on a clean tea towel.

4 Lightly butter 6 dariole moulds and line
with the cabbage leaves so they hang over
the edges. Fill each lined mould with the pepper
mixture until two-thirds full, then wrap the
overhanging cabbage leaves over the top to
make loose parcels. Loosely cover the top of
each parcel with foil, then place in a roasting
tin. Add hot water to the tin so that it comes
halfway up the sides of the dariole moulds.
Bake in the oven for 25–30 minutes until the
parcels are firm and bouncy to the touch.
Rest in a warm place until serving. Leave
the oven on.

5 For the ratatouille, sauté the aubergines in
a pan with the garlic in a little olive oil until
golden. Add the olives and basil and season to
taste. Set aside until serving.

6 For the aubergines à la Parmigiana , cut the aubergines into 5mm (¼in) thick slices, then sprinkle with salt and leave to rest for 10 minutes. Pat dry and deep fry in vegetable oil in batches at 180°C (350°F) until golden, then drain on kitchen paper and set aside. In another pan, prepare a tomato sauce. Gently fry the onion in a little olive oil until soft, then add the tomatoes. Cook for 20–25 minutes until reduced and thickened, then stir in the basil.

7 Place six 6cm (2½in) diameter, deep cooking rings onto a non-stick baking tray. Layer the fried aubergine slices, mozzarella cheese slices, tomato sauce, and Parmesan cheese inside the rings until full, seasoning to taste as you go. Bake for 30 minutes in the hot oven, until the cheese is bubbling and golden. Leave to rest for a few minutes before serving.

8 Meanwhile, place all the pesto ingredients into a food processor and blitz until smooth.

9 To serve, skewer the tomberries on 6 small skewers. Turn out the warm pepper bakes onto 6 warm serving plates. Put an aubergines à la Parmigiana stack alongside each. Add a spoonful of ratatouille and top with a tomberry skewer. Garnish the plates with a little micro cress and pea shoots, and serve immediately.

Wild mushroom and spinach tart with mustard leeks and fondant potato

Kennedy Leitch Ⓜ contestant

Preparation time 35 minutes   **Cooking time** 1 hour   **Serves 4**

For the pastry

150g (5½oz) unsalted butter, cubed

300g (10oz) plain flour

½ tsp salt

1 egg, plus 1 egg yolk, beaten

For the mushroom mix

25g (scant 1oz) dried porcini

100g (3½oz) butter

2 shallots, finely chopped

2 garlic cloves, crushed

800g (1¾lb) wild mushrooms (morels, girolles, ceps, chestnut etc.), cleaned and larger ones quartered or halved

100ml (3½fl oz) dry white wine

1 tbsp finely chopped thyme leaves

2 tsp truffle oil

75ml (2½fl oz) double cream, plus extra to taste

1 tbsp snipped chives

1 tbsp chopped tarragon

salt and freshly ground black pepper

For the fondant potato

2 large Désirée potatoes

100g (3½oz) unsalted butter

400ml (14fl oz) vegetable stock

2 garlic cloves

2 sprigs of thyme

For the leeks

50g (1¾oz) unsalted butter

2 tbsp olive oil

2 leeks, cut into 1cm (½in) lengths

100ml (3½fl oz) dry white wine

1 tbsp wholegrain mustard

For the spinach

knob of butter

1 garlic clove, crushed

150g (5½oz) spinach

Method

1 Preheat the oven to 180°C (350°F/Gas 4) and grease four 10–12cm (4–5in) loose-bottomed tartlet tins. Make the pastry by rubbing the butter and flour together with the salt. Slowly add the beaten egg to form a dough, adding 1–2 tbsp water if needed. Turn out onto a floured surface and knead until smooth. Wrap the pastry in cling film and chill in the fridge for 30 minutes. Roll out the pastry and use to line the greased tartlet tins. Place in the fridge for 10 minutes.

2 Line the uncooked pastry cases in the tartlet tins with greaseproof paper and fill with baking beans. Bake in the oven for 15 minutes, then remove the beans and paper and bake for a further 5 minutes. Cool slightly before filling.

3 Meanwhile, place the dried porcini for the mushroom mix in a bowl and cover with boiling water. Leave to soak for 20 minutes to rehydrate them, then strain, reserving the liquid.

4 Prepare the potatoes, Peel and halve the potatoes and cut into 4 equal-sized cylinder shapes, ensuring that the ends are flat. Heat the butter in a deep frying pan and add the potatoes, standing them on end. Fry until the undersides are golden, then add the stock, garlic, and thyme. Bring to the boil, then reduce to a simmer. Cover the pan with a piece of greaseproof paper and continue to simmer until the potatoes are tender. Set aside and keep warm until ready to serve.

5 Prepare the leeks. Heat the butter and oil in a pan and sauté the leek lengths until softened. Add the white wine and reduce by two-thirds, then stir in the mustard. Season and keep warm until needed.

6 For the mushroom mix, melt the butter in a pan, add the shallots and garlic, and cook for 2–3 minutes. Add all the mushrooms, including the soaked porcini, and cook until they begin to brown. Add the wine, thyme, and a little of the reserved porcini liquid. Cook until most of the wine has evaporated, then add the truffle oil and cook for 30 seconds. Stir in the cream, chives, and tarragon and season to taste.

7 For the spinach, gently heat the butter and garlic in a frying pan. Add the spinach, stir until wilted, then season to taste.

8 To finish the tarts, remove baked pastry cases from the tins, put a layer of spinach on the bottom of each, and top with the mushroom mix. Place a tart on each of the 4 serving plates and arrange the leeks and a potato next to them.

Ragoût of fish with cucumber and basil sauce and Parmesan twists

Christine Hamilton ⓜ Celebrity finalist

Preparation time 20 minutes **Cooking time** 35 minutes **Serves 4**

Ingredients

For the twists

125g (4½oz) all-butter puff pastry

1 egg, lightly beaten

20g (¾oz) Parmesan cheese, finely grated

large pinch of cayenne pepper

For the ragoût

20g (¾oz) butter

2 x 150g (5½oz) salmon fillets, skinned and left whole

150g (5½oz) monkfish fillet, skinned and cut into 3cm (1¼in) cubes

4 plump scallops, roes removed

12 large raw tiger prawns, peeled

salt and freshly ground black pepper

200ml (7fl oz) fish stock

75ml (2½fl oz) dry vermouth

100ml (3½fl oz) dry white wine

100ml (3½fl oz) double cream

10cm (4in) piece of cucumber, peeled, halved lengthways, deseeded, and sliced

20g (¾oz) basil leaves, chopped

½ lemon

125g (4½oz) samphire or fine asparagus

200g (7oz) long grain and wild rice, cooked

Method ↳

Method

1 Preheat the oven to 200°C (400°F/Gas 6). Lightly grease four 8cm (3in) ring moulds and place on a large baking tray, lined with baking parchment.

2 To make the twists, roll out the pastry on a floured surface to 30 x 12cm (12 x 5in). Brush with the beaten egg, and sprinkle over the cheese and cayenne pepper. Press the cheese into the pastry. Cut into 4 strips lengthways and twist each strip into a circle. Brush with more egg, then place a pastry circle into each of the prepared rings moulds on the baking tray. Cook in the oven for about 15 minutes, or until golden. Allow to cool a little, then remove the moulds. Set the twists aside until ready to serve.

TECHNIQUE

How to prepare fresh scallops

1 Scrub shell under cold running water before opening the scallop. Slide a knife between the top and bottom shell to open it, then carefully detach the scallop from the bottom shell with the knife.

2 Pull away and discard the viscera and frilled membrane. You can leave the cream and orange coral (roe) attached, or remove it too if you wish. Gently rinse the scallop in cold running water.

3 For the ragout, melt the butter in a large frying pan and add the salmon, monkfish, scallops, and prawns. Sprinkle with salt. Cook the fish for 3–4 minutes, turning once or twice, to cook through. Remove the monkfish, scallops, and prawns to a warming dish, cover in foil, and keep warm. Cook the salmon for a further 2–3 minutes, keeping it a little underdone in the middle. Gently flake and keep warm.

4 Add the fish stock to the pan, and boil until it has reduced by half. Add the vermouth, white wine, and cream, and boil again until it has reduced by about half and begins to thicken slightly. Strain the sauce to remove the cooking residues, and place back in the wiped out pan.

5 Add the sliced cucumber and gently cook for 2 minutes. Then add most of the basil, a good squeeze of lemon juice and seasoning to taste.

6 Steam the samphire or asparagus for about 2–3 minutes, and then strain.

7 To serve, place a portion of cooked rice in the centre of each of 4 serving plates, top with a Parmesan twist, and garnish with a sprig of basil. Spoon around the fish ragout, then spinkle over some steamed samphire or asparagus.

Roast cod and clams with bacon mash, creamy shallot sauce, and spinach

Sarah Whittle @ semi-finalist

Preparation time 1 hour 30 minutes   **Cooking time** 1 hour   **Serves 4**

Ingredients

4 thick cod fillets, 160g (5¾oz) each

plain flour, for dusting

sea salt and white pepper

75g (2½oz) unsalted butter

2 tbsp rapeseed oil

750g (1lb 10oz) baby spinach

For the bacon mash

6 rashers smoked dry-cure streaky bacon, rind removed

1.5kg (3lb 3oz) Maris Piper potatoes, cut into 8cm (3in) pieces

50g (1¾oz) unsalted butter

white pepper

For the shallot sauce

1kg (2¼lb) venus or palourde clams, scrubbed and soaked for 2 hours in salted water (use cockles if clams are unavailable)

½ large glass of dry white wine (nothing "oaky")

2 shallots or 1 small onion, very finely chopped

300ml (10fl oz) double cream

1 heaped tbsp thyme leaves

juice of ½ lemon

Method

Method

1 Preheat the oven to 180°C (350°F/Gas 4). Make the mash. Put the bacon on a non-stick baking tray in the oven for about 10 minutes until crisp. Cool and crumble, reserving a few rashers to garnish. Boil the potatoes for about 20 minutes until tender. Drain, return to the pan, add the butter and mash well. Season with pepper, stir in the crumbled bacon, then set aside and keep warm. Leave the oven on.

2 For the sauce, put the clams in a large pan with the wine and half the shallots or onion. Cook, covered, over high heat, shaking from time to time, for about 4–5 minutes, until the clams have opened – discard any that haven't. Drain into a colander over a bowl to catch the juice. Reserve 12 of the clams in their shells for garnish and shell the rest.

TECHNIQUE

How to shell clams

 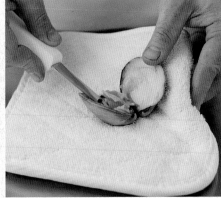

1 Clean clams under cold running water and discard any open ones. Place each clam in a towel to protect your fingers. Insert the tip of a sharp knife between the shell and twist to force apart.

2 Using the tip of your knife, sever the muscle that attaches the clam to its shell, and release the clam. If using soft-shell clams, remove and discard the dark membrane before serving.

3 Pour the clam juice into a pan and add the remaining shallot or onion. Simmer for 10 minutes until reduced slightly, then add the cream. Simmer for a further 5 minutes then, if you wish to, blend until smooth using a hand blender. Add the thyme and shelled clams and check the seasoning, adding a little lemon juice to taste. Set sauce aside and keep warm.

4 To cook the cod, dust the skin side with seasoned flour. Put 50g (1¾oz) butter and the oil in a non-stick ovenproof frying pan over medium heat until frothing. Put the fish in, skin-side down, and cook until the fish turns white halfway up its sides. Baste with the oil and butter once, then put it in the hot oven for 7–8 minutes or until opaque. Meanwhile, heat the remaining butter in another pan and add the washed baby spinach. Cook until wilted, then season and drain.

5 To serve, spoon warm mash onto each of 4 serving plates. Place 3 clams in their shells around each mound of mash, and top with the wilted spinach, then a fillet of cod, and some pieces of the reserved bacon. Pour the sauce around and over the top.

Chicken stuffed with wild mushrooms and hazelnuts with pan haggerty

David Hall Ⓜ semi-finalist

Preparation time 45 minutes   **Cooking time** 40 minutes   **Serves 4**

Ingredients

For the stuffing
2 tbsp butter

150g (5½oz) wild mushrooms, finely chopped

2 tbsp thyme leaves, finely chopped

50g (1¾oz) hazelnuts, coarsely chopped

2 chicken livers, finely chopped

2 tbsp finely chopped flat-leaf parsley

2 good-quality pork sausages, skin removed

salt and freshly ground black pepper

For the chicken
4 tbsp olive oil

4 chicken legs, boned, with skin on

For the pan haggerty
50g (1¾oz) butter

3 large Desirée potatoes, peeled and thinly sliced

200g (7oz) onion, thinly sliced

50g (1¾oz) Cheddar cheese, grated

For the gravy
400ml (14fl oz) fruity red wine

200ml (7fl oz) port

1 shallot, finely diced

1 tbsp balsamic vinegar

1 tbsp dried mushrooms, rehydrated

2 sprigs of thyme

1 bay leaf

400ml (14fl oz) chicken stock

50g (1¾oz) butter

For the caramelized turnip
1 turnip, diced

50g (1¾oz) butter

50g (1¾oz) light soft brown sugar

For the kale
300g (10oz) curly kale, shredded

50g (1¾oz) butter

Method

1 First make the stuffing. Heat butter in a non-stick pan. Add the mushrooms and cook gently for 5 minutes. Put in a bowl and mix with the thyme, hazelnuts, livers, parsley, and sausage meat. Season with salt and pepper. Drizzle 2 tbsp of olive oil onto 4 large squares of foil. Lay a boned chicken leg on each, skin side down. Season with salt and pepper and divide stuffing between the chicken legs. Roll the chicken around the stuffing, wrapping tightly in the foil. Twist the ends of the foil, so the chicken parcels resemble Christmas crackers.

2 Bring a large pan of water to the boil and add the chicken parcels to the pan. Simmer for 20 minutes, or until the chicken is cooked all the way through, then set aside and keep warm.

TECHNIQUE

How to bone a chicken drumstick

1 Holding the drumstick steady, and starting in the middle of the drumstick, insert the tip of your knife until you locate the bone. Slice along the bone in both directions to expose it fully.

2 Open the flesh out and using short strokes to minimise tearing, neatly cut around the bone to free it completely from the flesh. Discard the bone, or use it to make a stock.

3 Meanwhile, make the pan haggerty. Melt the butter in a large ovenproof frying pan, layer in the potato and onion and season with salt and pepper. Sprinkle over the grated cheese and cover with a tight-fitting lid. Simmer over a low heat for 20–25 minutes, or until potato is cooked.

4 For the gravy, bring the wine and port to the boil in a pan, with the shallot, vinegar, mushrooms, thyme, and bay leaf. Cook over a moderate heat for 15 minutes, until liquid has reduced by half. Add the chicken stock and simmer for 10 minutes to reduce by half again. Strain into a clean pan, and season with salt and pepper. Reheat, and then whisk in the butter. Set aside and keep warm.

5 For the turnip, bring a pan of water to the boil and simmer the turnip for 5 minutes, then drain. Melt the butter in a frying pan, add the sugar and turnip and shake the pan until the outside of the turnip is caramelized. Keep warm.

6 Remove chicken from foil. Heat 2tbsp olive oil in a frying pan. Add chicken and cook for 2 minutes, until crisp and golden. Keep warm.

7 When the pan haggerty is cooked, remove the lid and place the pan under a hot grill until the cheese is bubbling and golden.

8 To cook the kale, simmer for 3–4 minutes in a pan of salted water. Drain well and return to the pan. Add the butter, season, and mix well.

9 To serve, slice the chicken and arrange on 4 warm serving plates with some pan haggerty, caramelized turnip, and kale. Finish by drizzling some gravy around the plate.

Sumac and thyme-roasted chicken with saffron jus, and pimentón-roast potatoes

Matthew Driver @ contestant

Preparation time 10 minutes   **Cooking time** 40 minutes   **Serves 4**

For the chicken

4 chicken supremes, skin on

1 tbsp sumac, plus extra to garnish

leaves from 2 sprigs of thyme, chopped

2 garlic cloves, crushed

2 tbsp olive oil

salt and freshly ground black pepper

For the potatoes

4 Maris piper potatoes, peeled and cut into small cubes

1 tbsp smoked paprika

2 tbsp olive oil

For the jus

500ml (16fl oz) fresh chicken stock

pinch of saffron

125g (4½oz) very cold unsalted butter, cubed

To serve

350g (12oz) French beans, trimmed

1 tbsp olive oil

1 tbsp finely chopped flat-leaf parsley

½ tsp finely chopped garlic

TECHNIQUE

How to joint a chicken

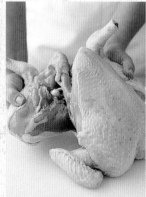

1 To remove the wishbone, scrape the flesh away from it, using a sharp knife, then twist it with your fingers and discard.

2 With the chicken breast-side up on a board, use a sharp knife to cut through the thigh joint and separate the leg from the rest of the bird.

3 Now pull the leg back to dislocate the leg joint. You should hear a distinct popping sound when the ball separates from the socket.

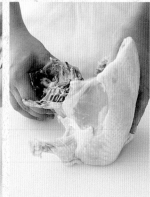

4 If there is any skin or meat still attached to the bird's body, use your knife to free it. Repeat steps 2 and 3 to remove the other leg.

5 Pull the wing straight, then cut through the middle joint with poultry shears to remove the winglet. Repeat for the other winglet.

6 Now grasp the backbone with your hands and firmly pull it away from the upper part of the body (the 2 breasts and wings).

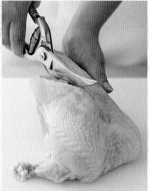

7 To remove the lower end of the backbone, use poultry shears to cut it away from the remaining body.

8 Starting at the neck, use poultry shears to cut all the way through the backbone to separate the breasts.

9 The chicken is now cut into 4 pieces. Any leftover bones (such as the backbone) can be used to make stock.

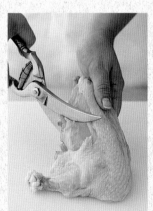

10 Use poultry shears to cut each breast in half diagonally, producing one breast and one wing. Repeat to separate the other breast.

11 Cut each leg through the knee joint (above the drumstick) that connects to the thigh, and cut through to separate.

12 Now, there are two drumsticks, two thighs, two wings, and two breasts. The chicken is divided into 8 pieces.

Method

1 Preheat the oven to 200°C (400°F/Gas 6). Trim and score the chicken and place in a bowl with the sumac, thyme, garlic, olive oil, and salt and pepper. Ensure the chicken is coated in the mixture, then leave to marinate for at least 30 minutes.

2 Pat the potato cubes dry on kitchen paper and season with smoked paprika (pimentón), salt, and pepper. Add the olive oil to a roasting tin, then add the potato cubes and place in the oven for 20–25 minutes, until crisp and golden brown.

3 Meanwhile, set a frying pan on high heat. Rub the marinated chicken with a little extra oil and sear skin-side down in the pan for 5 minutes until the skin begins to crisp. Remove from the pan, dip in a little more sumac mixture, and place in a roasting tin. Roast in the hot oven, skin-side up, for 15 minutes. Transfer to a warm plate and leave to rest.

4 While the chicken is roasting, make the jus. Bring the chicken stock and saffron to the boil in a small pan, then cook until syrupy and reduced by three-quarters. Gradually whisk in the cold cubed butter until thickened. Season to taste and keep warm.

5 Bring a large pan of salted water to the boil, add the beans, and cook for 3 minutes, until just tender. Drain and toss with the olive oil, parsley, garlic, and some seasoning.

6 To serve, carve each piece of chicken in half, sprinkle with a little sumac, and serve with the potatoes, beans, and saffron jus.

Roasted salmon with clams, broad bean purée, and horseradish broth

Alice Churchill ⓜ **Professionals semi-finalist**

Preparation time 1 hour 10 minutes   **Cooking time** 50 minutes   **Serves 4**

Ingredients

300g (10oz) frozen broad beans

sea salt and freshly ground white pepper

1 small onion, diced

3 fennel bulbs, cut into eighths

2 tbsp grated horseradish

300ml (10fl oz) whipping cream

100ml (3½fl oz) crème fraîche

600g (1lb 5oz) salmon, skin on and cut into 12 even-sized pieces

24 clams

300ml (10fl oz) white wine

300g (10oz) baby carrots

6 small turnips, cut into quarters

25g (scant 1oz) butter

small handful of flat-leaf parsley, chopped

Method

1 Preheat the oven to 200°C (400°F/Gas 6). Boil the beans in salted water for 3–4 minutes, or until soft. Drain, then blitz beans to a purée with a blender or in a food processor. Sieve and season well.

2 Sweat the onion in a pan with the fennel. Add horseradish, then add the cream and crème fraîche, and allow the broth to reduce for 10–15 minutes, until thickened. Season well and set aside. Then reheat and whisk lightly to make it frothy just before serving.

3 Place salmon in a roasting tin, skin-side up, and roast in the preheated oven for 10 minutes.

4 Simmer the clams and wine in a pan for 5 minutes, or until clams have all fully opened. Boil carrots and turnips in lightly salted water for 5 minutes. Melt the butter in a small pan and add the parsley. Reheat bean purée

5 Divide salmon and clams between 4 serving plates, toss vegetables in the parsley butter and place alongside with bean purée. Spoon over the hot broth.

Spiced blackened poussin with aubergine raita and wholewheat puffs

Perveen Nekoo @ quarter-finalist

Preparation time 25 minutes   **Cooking time** 50 minutes   **Serves 4**

Ingredients

2 poussins

2 tbsp toasted sesame seeds

For the marinade

4 tbsp tomato purée

1 bunch of spring onions, finely chopped

2 garlic cloves

5cm (2in) piece of fresh root ginger, grated

4 tsp ground cumin

2 tbsp toasted sesame seeds

2 tsp ground cinnamon

2 tsp sweet paprika

2 green bird's eye chillies

salt and freshly ground black pepper

4 tbsp olive oil

For the raita

1 medium purple aubergine, cut into small cubes

2 tbsp sunflower oil

1 tsp ground cumin

1 tsp cumin seeds

2 tsp clear honey

300ml (10fl oz) Greek-style yogurt

15cm (6in) piece of cucumber, finely diced

200g (7oz) red onion, finely diced

10 vine-ripened cherry tomatoes, quartered

20g (¾oz) mint, chopped

For the wholewheat puffs

60g (2oz) wholemeal flour

250ml (8fl oz) sunflower oil

Method

1 Preheat the oven to 200ºC (400ºF/Gas 6). Put all the marinade ingredients in a bowl and blitz using a hand blender, until the mixture resembles a thick paste. Spread all over the poussins, place them in a roasting tin and roast in the hot oven for 50 minutes. Remove from the oven and sprinkle with sesame seeds. Leave the oven on.

2 To make the raita, season the aubergine and toss in a little oil. Roast for 15–20 minutes in the hot oven until the aubergine is golden on the outside and soft to the touch. Remove from the oven and toss in the ground cumin and cumin seeds. Drizzle with honey, return to the oven for 5 minutes and then set aside.

3 Place the yogurt in a bowl and stir in the cucumber, red onion, tomatoes, and mint. Season with salt and pepper then layer with the aubergine into a small serving dish. Refrigerate until needed.

4 To make the wholewheat puffs, place the flour, 1 tsp oil, 3 tbsp water and salt in a bowl and mix with a palette knife to form a dough. Place the dough on a lightly floured board and knead for 2 minutes. Roll out and cut out 12 circles using a 8cm (3in) round cutter.

5 Heat the remaining oil in a pan and deep-fry the wholewheat puffs for 30–45 seconds on each side or until each one puffs up. Drain on kitchen paper and serve immediately with the poussins and raita.

Harissa pan-fried cod with roasted roots and a fresh coriander sauce

Matt James ⓜ Celebrity quarter-finalist

Preparation time 1 hour **Cooking time** 30 minutes **Serves 4**

Ingredients

3 large King Edward potatoes, peeled and sliced into finger-sized chips

2 large carrots, sliced into finger-sized chips

2 medium parsnips, sliced into finger-sized chips

2 tbsp extra virgin olive oil

sea salt and freshly ground black pepper

4 pieces of cod loin, 175g (6oz) each, boned but not skinned

4 tsp harissa paste

lemon slices, to garnish

For the sauce

1 medium onion, finely diced

1 garlic clove, finely diced

knob of butter

large glass of medium-dry white wine

300ml (10fl oz) double cream

1 bunch of coriander, finely chopped

Method

1 Preheat the oven to 180°C (350°F/Gas 4). Parboil the potatoes, carrots, and parsnips in salted water for 10 minutes, drain, then spread on a baking tray. Drizzle over 1 tbsp olive oil and sea salt, then place in the hot oven. Roast until golden brown, turning occasionally.

2 Meanwhile, heat remaining oil in an ovenproof frying pan. Season cod on both sides, then smear harissa paste on the fleshy side. Place skin-side down in the pan. Fry for 4–5 minutes, flip over and cook for 2 minutes before placing the pan in the hot oven, on shelf below the roasting vegetables, for 6 minutes.

3 For the sauce, sweat onion and garlic in a small pan with the butter until soft. Add wine, simmer for 4–5 minutes, then stir in the cream. Warm through, and add the coriander. Serve cod skin-side up on a pile of roasted roots. Pour over the sauce and garnish with lemon slices.

Spiced magret of duck with roasted root vegetables

Michael Pajak @ quarter-finalist

Preparation time 30 minutes   **Cooking time** 40–45 minutes   **Serves 4**

Ingredients

4 duck breasts, at room temperature

1 tbsp ground ginger

1 tbsp coriander seeds

1 star anise

1 tbsp Sichuan peppercorns

1 tsp ground cinnamon

2 tbsp sherry, apple, or cider vinegar

250ml (8fl oz) apple juice

30g (1oz) unsalted butter, chilled

For the vegetables

2 carrots

2 parsnips

½ swede

4 baby beetroots

4 baby turnips

2 onions, red or white

olive oil, to drizzle

salt and freshly ground black pepper

5–6 bay leaves

few sprigs of rosemary

Method

1 Preheat the oven to 180°C (350°F/Gas 4). Chop the vegetables to a size where they will all cook evenly: leave thin carrots or parsnips whole, cut thick ones lengthways, halve and cut into 2.5cm (1in) dice; cut the swede into 2.5cm (1in) dice; trim the beetroots and turnips but leave whole. Quarter the onions, leaving the root end attached.

2 Put vegetables in a large roasting tin. Drizzle with olive oil and toss to coat evenly. Season with salt, and add the bay leaves and rosemary. Cook in the hot oven, turning once or twice, until tender and golden – about 40–45 minutes. Check the seasoning and add a little pepper.

3 Meanwhile, cook the duck breasts. Grind all the spices as finely as you can. Score the skin of the duck with a sharp knife and rub the spice mix all over the breast. Put duck, skin-side down, in a cold frying pan (preferably ovenproof), bring up to medium-high heat and cook for about 10 minutes.

4 Season the flesh side with salt and pepper, and put the frying pan in the preheated oven for about 8 minutes until cooked to medium rare. If you do not have a suitable pan, add the duck to the roasting vegetables.

5 Take the frying pan from the oven, remove the duck and allow it to rest while you make the sauce. Pour off some fat from the pan and place on medium heat. Add the vinegar to deglaze the pan. Scrape the bottom and let the vinegar reduce by two-thirds. Add the apple juice and let it reduce by about one-third. Remove the pan from the heat, whisk in the chilled butter and check the seasoning.

6 Divide the roasted vegetables between 4 serving plates. Either slice up the duck breasts into about 5 thick slices and fan out over the vegetables, or serve whole. Pour over a little of the sauce and serve.

Herb-marinated salmon in coconut curry sauce

Andy Oliver @ finalist

Preparation time 10 minutes   **Cooking time** 15 minutes   **Serves 4**

Ingredients

4 pieces of salmon fillet, about 150g (5½oz) each, skinned

For the marinade

1 onion, roughly chopped

2 tsp grated fresh root ginger

4 garlic cloves, roughly chopped

3 medium-hot green chillies, roughly chopped

2 tsp ground turmeric

2 tsp ground coriander

4 tsp garam masala

handful of coriander leaves

handful of mint leaves

3 tbsp Greek yogurt

For the sauce

1 tsp sunflower oil

400ml (14fl oz) coconut milk

1 tbsp thick tamarind paste

200g (7oz) baby spinach, washed

salt and freshly ground black pepper

Method

1 Preheat the oven to 200°C (400°F/Gas 6).

2 Make the marinade by blitzing the onion, ginger, garlic, and chillies in a food processor with a good pinch of salt and 1 tbsp of water to help bind the paste. Mix in the ground spices.

3 Take out half this paste and set aside. Add the coriander and mint leaves to the paste left in the food processor, reserving some to garnish. Whizz again until smooth. Mix in the yogurt and rub the mixture over the salmon. Leave for 30 minutes.

4 Place the salmon on a greased baking tray and cook in the hot oven for 5–10 minutes, depending on the thickness.

5 Meanwhile, make the sauce. Fry remaining paste in the oil for 3 minutes, then add the coconut milk and 4 tbsp of water. Simmer for 5 minutes then add the tamarind paste and spinach. Season to taste and cook spinach until wilted.

6 To serve, spoon the curry sauce into wide bowls and place the salmon fillets on top. Garnish with the reserved coriander and mint leaves.

Spicy chicken with plantain

Darren Campbell MBE @ Celebrity contestant

Preparation time 20 minutes   **Cooking time** 45 minutes   **Serves 4**

Ingredients

For the chicken

4 chicken breasts, with skin on

juice of 1 lemon

2 tbsp olive oil

1 tbsp Schwartz Season-All

2 tbsp Schwartz No Added Salt Chicken Seasoning

1 tbsp curry powder

2 onions, chopped

3 garlic cloves, crushed

1 tbsp chopped thyme leaves

1 red chilli, deseeded and finely chopped

1 green chilli, deseeded and finely chopped

1 red pepper, deseeded and chopped

1 yellow pepper, deseeded and chopped

1 green pepper, deseeded and chopped

3 tbsp tomato purée

a small handful of coriander, chopped

For the plantain

1 large ripe plantain

1 tbsp olive oil

For the rice

200g (7oz) basmati rice

2 cloves

1 bay leaf

1 tsp olive oil

Method →

Method

1 Wash the chicken breasts in lemon juice, and set aside. Add olive oil, seasoning, and curry powder to a frying pan and fry over medium heat. Allow the flavours to gently fuse together. Add the onions, garlic, thyme, chilli peppers, and peppers and fry for a few minutes until soft.

2 Increase the heat to high, add the chicken and fry until browned. Turn the heat down and add water to halfway up the chicken breasts. Cover and simmer for 20 minutes, then add the tomato purée. Cook for a further 10 minutes until the chicken is cooked through. Remove the chicken from the sauce and leave to rest. Finish the sauce with the coriander. Set aside.

3 Cut the tips off both ends of the plantain. Make 4 lengthways slices through the skin from one end to the other. Peel the skin from the flesh sideways, cut the peeled plantain in thirds crossways, and then cut each piece in half lengthways. Heat the oil in a pan over medium heat, add the plantain, and cook until golden. Keep warm.

4 Wash the rice until the water runs clear. Place rice and 300ml (10fl oz) water in a pan with the cloves, bay leaf, and olive oil. Bring to the boil, then cover, and reduce the heat to the lowest setting. Cook for 10 minutes, then remove from the heat, leaving the lid on, and leave to stand for a further 10 minutes. Remove the cloves and bay leaf and fluff up rice with a fork.

5 To serve, mound the rice on 4 warmed plates. Top with 3 plantain slices. Diagonally slice the chicken, and place on top. To finish, reheat the sauce, then spoon over, and serve immediatcly.

Thai green chicken curry

Nargis Chaudhary Ⓜ semi-finalist

Preparation time 30 minutes   **Cooking time** 50 minutes   **Serves 4**

Ingredients

1–2 tbsp vegetable oil

2 x 400g cans coconut milk

400g (14oz) chicken breast and thighs, skinless and boneless, cut into cubes

1 aubergine, cut into 8 large cubes

210g jar pea aubergines, drained

15g (½oz) fresh root ginger, grated

small handful of lime leaves

1 tsp palm, gran, or granulated sugar

1 tbsp nam pla (Thai fish sauce)

salt

225g (8oz) Thai jasmine rice

knob of butter

For the curry paste

1 tbsp coriander seeds

1 tbsp white peppercorns

1 tbsp cumin seeds

50g (1¾oz) green bird's eye chillies, deseeded and chopped

50g (1¾oz) long green chillies, deseeded and chopped

2 red chillies, deseeded and chopped

1 garlic bulb, cloves peeled

3 lemongrass stalks

3 tsp ground turmeric

handful of coriander

60g (2oz) galangal, grated

8 red or white shallots, chopped

grated zest of 1 lime

30g (1oz) shrimp paste

To serve

basil leaves

red chillies, left whole

Method

1 For the curry paste, grind the coriander seeds, peppercorns, and cumin to a fine powder in a pestle and mortar, then blitz with the remaining ingredients to form a smooth paste.

2 Heat oil in a large pan or wok and add 4 tbsp of the curry paste. Cook, stirring, over a medium heat until it smells fragrant. Stir in 2–3 tbsp coconut milk and cook for 5 minutes. Stir in the remaining coconut milk.

3 Add the chicken with the fresh and drained aubergines. Simmer for 15 minutes, then stir in the rest of the ingredients and cook for another 5 minutes. Taste and add salt if necessary.

4 Meanwhile, cook the rice following packet instructions Stir in a knob of butter.

5 Garnish curry with basil leaves and red chillies, and serve with the buttered rice.

Pork bafat with okra pachadi and rice bread

Michelle Peters Ⓜ semi-finalist

Preparation time 20 minutes   **Cooking time** 1 hour 45 minutes   **Serves 4**

Ingredients

500g (1lb 2oz) shoulder pork, diced

4 large onions, chopped

2 tbsp tomato ketchup

For the marinade

25g (scant 1oz) tamarind

60ml (2fl oz) boiling water

2 tbsp bafat powder

1 tsp garam masala

½ tsp ground nutmeg

8cm (3in) piece root ginger, chopped

2 garlic cloves, chopped

2 bay leaves, torn

5 green chillies, chopped

pinch of salt

100ml (3½fl oz) red wine vinegar

5 cloves, 5 cardamom pods, and 2.5cm (1in) piece of cinnamon tied in muslin

For the okra pachadi

1 tbsp vegetable oil

1 tsp black gram

1 tsp mustard seeds

1 tsp cumin seeds

3 mild dried red chillies, finely chopped

1 tsp Bengal gram (split yellow peas)

sprig of curry leaves

8 okra, chopped

200g (7oz) plain yogurt

For the rice bread (sanna)

250g (9oz) idli rice or pudding rice

70g (2¼oz) basmati rice

25g (scant 1oz) beaten rice (optional)

45g (1½oz) cleaned white urad dal

3 tbsp sugar

1 tsp yeast dissolved in 2 tbsp warm water

Method

1 Prepare sanna batter a day ahead. Put idli, basmati and beaten rice with urad dal in a bowl. Cover with cold water and leave for about 4 hours. Drain, then grind the soaked mixture with the sugar and a pinch of salt, using a coffee grinder or blender, with enough water to achieve a consistency like double cream. Pour batter into a clean bowl, and stir in the yeast. Leave in a warm place for at least 4 hours, to rise.

2 Soak the tamarind in the boiling water for 20–30 minutes, breaking up the block as it softens. Strain paste into a bowl. Add the pork, 200ml (7fl oz) water, and remaining marinade ingredients. Leave for about 1 hour. Transfer the pork and the marinade to a pan, cover and cook gently for 1 hour 15 minutes, without adding any more water. Mix in the chopped onions halfway through the cooking time. Stir in the ketchup and simmer for another 30 minutes until the pork is tender, adding water if necessary.

3 To cook the okra, heat the oil in a heavy frying pan and add the rest of the ingredients except the yogurt. Cook over a low heat for about 20 minutes or until the okra is soft. Add salt to taste and then the yogurt.

4 To steam the sannas, grease four 150ml (5fl oz) ramekins with a little vegetable oil. Fill each ramekin one-third full with the prepared sanna batter. Steam in a steamer for 8 minutes. To check sannas are ready, poke a cocktail stick into one – it should not have wet batter sticking to it. Carefully turn sannas out of the ramakins and leave to cool slightly. Remove the bay leaves and spices in muslin from the pork and serve with the okra and warm rice bread.

Spiced squash soup with Parmesan croutons

Caroline Brewester ⓜ finalist

Preparation time 45 minutes **Cooking time** 30 minutes **Serves 4**

Ingredients

1 medium butternut squash, peeled, deseeded, and cut into slices 1cm (½in) thick

2 tbsp sunflower oil, plus extra for greasing

15g (½oz) salted butter

1 onion, finely chopped

1 medium potato, peeled and diced

1 tsp ground coriander

1 tsp ground cumin

½ fresh red chilli, or more to taste, finely chopped

600ml (1 pint) hot vegetable stock, plus extra if needed

60ml (2fl oz) double cream

salt and freshly ground black pepper

For the parmesan croutons

2 thick slices slightly stale white bread, crusts removed

15g (½oz) Parmesan cheese, freshly grated

Method

1 Preheat the oven to 200°C (400°F/Gas 6). Grease a large baking tray. Brush squash with 1 tbsp oil. Lay on baking sheet and roast in oven for about 10 minutes, until browned on the bottom. Turn over and roast for 10–15 minutes, until soft.

2 Meanwhile, melt butter in a pan over a low heat. Add the onion and potato and cook, stirring occasionally, until onion is translucent and the potato has softened. Add coriander, cumin, and chilli and cook for 2 minutes. Cut roasted squash into chunks and add to the pan. Pour in the stock, to just cover vegetables.

Bring to the boil, then simmer for 15 minutes. Cool slightly then blitz with a hand blender until smooth. Return to the pan, and add the cream plus extra stock if the soup is very thick. Season and reheat gently.

3 For the croutons, preheat the grill to high. Cut bread into 1cm (½in) cubes and stir with remaining oil in a bowl. Put bread cubes on a baking tray and grill for 1 minute, until golden brown. Turn over and grill for another minute, then sprinkle over Parmesan and grill again until golden. Serve the soup with croutons on top.

Pepper-stuffed pork with aubergine purée, choi sum, and aromatic ginger sauce

Simon Small ⓜ quarter-finalist

Preparation time 1 hour   **Cooking time** 1 hour 45 minutes   **Serves 4**

Ingredients

1kg (2¼lb) lean loin of pork on the bone, with a good layer of fatty skin

salt and freshly ground black pepper

1 tsp five-spice powder

For the stuffing

1 tbsp groundnut oil, plus extra for frying

1 tbsp sesame oil

1 red pepper, halved and deseeded

1 orange pepper, halved and deseeded

1 yellow pepper, halved and deseeded

1 tbsp chopped coriander

½ tsp sesame seeds

For the aubergine purée

2 large aubergines, halved lengthways

1 tbsp groundnut oil

1 tbsp sesame oil

½ tsp five-spice powder

For the sauce

150ml (5fl oz) red wine

75ml (2½fl oz) rice wine

2 tbsp rice wine vinegar

3 tbsp shiitake extract

2 tbsp dark soy sauce

2 tbsp dark soft brown sugar

3 star anise

1 stalk lemongrass

2 garlic cloves

4 kaffir lime leaves

½ tsp dried chilli flakes

4 spring onions, sliced into 2cm (¾in) lengths

10cm (4in) piece fresh root ginger, roughly peeled and cut into strips

To serve

1 tsp sesame seeds

2 large stalks choi sum, quartered

1 mild red chilli, thinly sliced

Method

Method

1 Preheat the oven to 230°C (450°F/Gas 8). Prepare the pork by removing the bone to enable it to be stuffed. Carefully remove the skin from the remaining meat, retaining the fat. Score the skin, rub in salt, and sprinkle with the five-spice powder. Place skin in a roasting tin and roast in the hot oven for about 1 hour until crispy. Remove from the oven and leave to cool. Cut into matchsticks and set aside.

2 Meanwhile start preparing the stuffing. Mix the groundnut and sesame oils in a bowl and use to brush the peppers. Season with salt and place them skin-side up on a baking tray. Cook in the hot oven for about 25 minutes or until the skins have blackened. When cool enough to handle, peel off and discard the skin, and slice the peppers. Set aside.

TECHNIQUE

How to prepare lemongrass

1 Use a very sharp kitchen knife to cut off the upper part of the lemongrass stem. Discard.

2 Crush the lower part of the lemongrass stem using the back of a heavy knife or a wooden kitchen mallet.

3 Repeat the process with the aubergines for the purée, but place skin-side down and score some of the flesh to allow the oils and salt to penetrate. Put in the oven for 25 minutes until soft. Remove from the oven and leave to cool.

4 Reduce the the oven to 190°C (375°F/Gas 5). To finish the stuffing, mix the roasted sliced peppers, coriander, and sesame seeds together, then season. Lay stuffing in the centre of the open pork loin, roll, and tie up with string. Heat a frying pan to hot, add the pork and sear on all sides. Transfer to a roasting tin and roast in the oven for 35–45 minutes, until there are no pink juices. Remove from the oven and leave to rest.

5 When the aubergines are cool enough to handle, scoop out the flesh and mash up with the five-spice powder. Pass through a sieve, season with salt and pepper, and keep warm.

6 To make the sauce, pour the red wine into a medium-sized saucepan and then add the remaining ingredients, reserving a little of the ginger. Bring to the boil, reduce the heat and simmer until reduced by three-quarters.

7 Heat a small frying pan over a medium-high heat, toss in the 1 tsp sesame seeds and toast them. Remove from the pan, then toss in and lightly toast the remaining ginger. Set aside. Stir-fry the choi sum in some groundnut oil.

8 To serve, put some aubergine purée in the centre of 4 serving plates. Place the choi sum around the aubergine and slice 2 rounds of pork and place on top. Strain the sauce and spoon plenty over the dish. Dress the pork with the toasted sesame seeds and ginger strips, chilli slices, and matchsticks of crispy pork skin.

Thai beef massaman curry with jasmine rice

Alix Carwood ⓜ quarter-finalist

Preparation time 25 minutes   **Cooking time** 55 minutes   **Serves 4**

Ingredients

10 cardamom pods

5 cloves

3 tbsp vegetable oil

450g (1lb) lean rump steak, cut into bite-sized chunks

400ml can coconut milk

2 tbsp nam pla Thai fish sauce)

175ml (6fl oz) beef stock

60g (2oz) unsalted, skinned peanuts

1 large Maris Piper potato, peeled and cut into chunks

1cm (½in) piece fresh root ginger

1–2 tbsp palm sugar

1–2 tbsp tamarind paste

For the curry paste

1 red chilli

1 stalk of lemongrass

1cm (½in) galangal or 1 tsp galangal in sunflower oil

5 cloves

1 cinnamon stick

10 cardamom pods

3 garlic cloves

3 shallots

large handful of coriander

olive oil

To serve

300g (10oz) jasmine rice

salt

unsalted, skinned peanuts

coriander leaves, to garnish

Method

Method

1 To make the curry paste, put all the ingredients in a food processor with a little olive oil and blend until they form a paste.

2 For the beef curry, put the cardamom and cloves in a large casserole and dry-fry to release the fragrance. Remove and set aside.

3 Put a little of the vegetable oil in the casserole and fry 5 tbsp of the curry paste over medium heat for 5 minutes until the fragrance is released. Add the beef and fry until browned. Then add the toasted cardamon and cloves and the rest of the curry ingredients and paste, and bring to the boil. Reduce to a simmer and cook for about 45 minutes until the beef is tender and the sauce is syrupy and reduced. Keep warm.

TECHNIQUE

How to prepare fresh root ginger

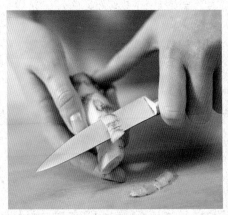 

1 Peel as much of the fresh root as you need, cutting off any woody or dry bits.

2 Using a sharp knife, slice the root thinly across the grain into a series of fine discs.

4 Bring a large pan of water to the boil. Add a pinch of salt and then the jasmine rice. Reduce the heat and leave to simmer for about 10 minutes until the rice is cooked through.

5 Divide the curry between 4 warmed serving bowls and sprinkle over the peanuts. Place a portion of jasmine rice alongside, garnished with coriander leaves.

3 Stack the discs, press down firmly, and shred them into fine slivers.

4 Line up the slivers and cut them across to chop. To chop more finely, mound up the pieces and chop again.

Roasted rack of venison with grand veneur sauce and root vegetables

Andi Peters ⓜ Celebrity finalist

Preparation time 20 minutes   **Cooking time** 50 minutes   **Serves** 4

Ingredients

900g (2lb) 8-bone venison rack, French trimmed, with the trimmings reserved

2 tbsp olive oil

25g (scant 1oz) stale white breadcrumbs

1 tbsp chopped thyme

1 tbsp chopped rosemary

1 tbsp Dijon mustard

For the root vegetables

2 parsnips, peeled and finely diced

2 carrots, finely diced

150g (5½oz) celeriac, finely diced

2 small turnips, finely diced

2 tbsp olive oil

salt and freshly ground black pepper

For the grand veneur sauce

25g (scant 1oz) butter

20g (¾oz) diced carrot

1 shallot, chopped

1 celery stick, finely chopped

20g (¾oz) chopped leek

sprig of thyme

1 bay leaf

8 black peppercorns

20g (¾oz) tomato purée

2 tbsp red wine vinegar

250ml (8fl oz) dry red wine

120ml (4fl oz) hot water

1 tbsp redcurrant jelly

1 tbsp double cream

1 tsp butter

Method

1 Preheat the oven to 200°C (400°F/Gas 6). To roast the vegetables, place them in a roasting tin and pour over the oil, season well and toss to coat with oil. Roast in the oven for 45–50 minutes, turning over once or twice during cooking to ensure browning on all sides.

2 Season the venison rack and heat half the oil in a large frying pan. When hot, add the rack and sear for 3 minutes on each side. Transfer to a roasting tin, bone-side down, and cook in the hot oven for 10 minutes.

3 Meanwhile, toast the breadcrumbs in the oven for 5–7 minutes, turning once to ensure even browning. Then blend in a food processor with the thyme, rosemary, seasoning, and the remaining oil.

4 Remove the venison from the oven and brush with mustard, avoiding the bones. Then roll in the breadcrumb mix, return to the oven and cook for 8 minutes for medium. Remove from the oven and leave to rest.

5 To make the sauce, melt the butter in a casserole dish. Add the vegetables and leave to sweat for 5 minutes. Mix in the thyme, bay leaf, peppercorns, and tomato purée and cook for 4 minutes. Deglaze the pan with the vinegar and reduce until almost dry. Add the wine and reduce by half. Then add the water and reduce again until the sauce coats the back of a spoon. Remove the herbs and strain the sauce. To finish, gently whisk in the redcurrant jelly, double cream, and butter.

6 To serve, carve the rack into 4 pieces. Arrange on a bed of the roasted root vegetables and finish by pouring over the sauce.

Poached salmon in an Asian broth

inspired by **Mat Follas** @ champion

Preparation time 25 minutes   **Cooking time** 35 minutes   **Serves 4**

Ingredients

1 litre (1¾ pints) fish stock

2 lemongrass stalks, chopped

2.5cm (1in) piece of galangal or fresh root ginger, sliced into matchsticks

1 banana shallot, sliced

3–4 bird's eye chillies, deseeded and finely chopped

1 tsp golden caster sugar

¼ tsp salt

4 kaffir lime leaves, roughly shredded

1 tbsp nam pla (Thai fish sauce)

4 salmon fillets, 175g (6oz) each, skinned

2 heads of pak choi, quartered lengthways

juice of 1 lime

1 handful of coriander leaves, roughly chopped

Method

1 Bring the stock to the boil in a large saucepan with the lemongrass, galangal or ginger, shallot, chillies, sugar, salt, and 2 of the lime leaves. Simmer for 10–15 minutes.

2 Stir in the nam pla, then gently lower in the salmon, followed by the pak choi, and turn the heat down to low. Cover with a lid and poach for 8–10 minutes. Remove the fish and pak choi and place in 4 warmed serving bowls.

3 Stir the remaining lime leaves, lime juice, and coriander leaves into the pan and taste for seasoning. Ladle the broth over the salmon and pak choi . Serve, with cooked noodles if desired.

Visual
Feasts

Saag paneer on a pumpkin rösti with tamarind glaze and coconut cream

Jackie Kearney Ⓜ **finalist**

Preparation time 50 minutes   **Cooking time** 35 minutes   **Serves 4**

Ingredients

For the rösti

1 small pumpkin, deseeded and peeled

1 large potato, peeled

1 green chilli, deseeded and finely diced

1 red chilli, deseeded and finely diced

small bunch of coriander, finely chopped

salt and freshly ground black peper

2 tbsp sunflower oil

For the saag paneer

500g (1lb 2oz) baby spinach

sunflower oil

4 tbsp ghee

1 tsp black mustard seeds

1 tsp cumin seeds

1 small white onion, finely sliced

1 green chilli, deseeded and finely diced

1 red chilli, deseeded and finely diced

½ tbsp ginger paste

1 tbsp garlic paste

2 tbsp garam masala

12 cherry tomatoes, halved

500g (1lb 2oz) paneer, cut into 4cm (1½in) cubes

For the tamarind glaze

2 tbsp sugar

2 tbsp red wine vinegar

100g (3½oz) tamarind paste

For the coconut cream

100g (3½oz) creamed coconut

3 tbsp warm water

To garnish

4 small coriander leaves

4–8 edible flowers

Method

1 Preheat the oven to 180°C (350°F/Gas 4). For the röstis, use a coarse grater to grate both the pumpkin and potato into a large bowl. Add the green and red chillies and the coriander. Season.

2 Heat the oil over medium to high heat in a large frying pan. Remove excess liquid from the rösti mixture by squeezing in a clean tea towel over the sink. Shape the mixture into 4 equal-sized patties. Carefully place in the hot oil and fry on both sides for about 3 minutes, or until lightly golden. Transfer to a baking tray and place in the hot oven for about 15 minutes, or until fully cooked.

3 Meanwhile, make the saag paneer. Bring a large pan of water to the boil and add the spinach. Blanch for about 30 seconds. Drain immediately and rinse under cold water. Purée the spinach with either a hand-held blender or in a food processor, adding salt and a little sunflower oil if needed. Set aside.

4 Melt 3 tbsp of the ghee in a saucepan over medium heat. Add the seeds and fry for 1 minute, stirring. Reduce the heat, add the onions, and fry for 4–5 minutes until softened.

5 Add both the chillies, and the ginger and garlic pastes, and continue to cook for 2–3 minutes until the garlic and ginger are both golden, taking care not to let them burn. Sprinkle in the garam masala and cook for 1 minute.

6 Finally add the spinach purée and tomatoes, and cook, stirring, for a further 2–3 minutes, until all the flavours are amalgamated.

7 In a separate pan, heat the remaining ghee over medium to high heat. Once melted, fry the paneer pieces until golden around the edges. Do this in batches if necessary. Once fried, transfer paneer with a slotted spoon to kitchen paper to drain off excess oil. Keep warm until ready to serve.

8 Make the tamarind glaze. Place all the ingredients in a saucepan with a little water and boil over high heat until reduced by about two-thirds and syrupy. Strain through a fine sieve to reach a smooth consistency. Transfer to a squeezy bottle, ready to use for garnishing.

9 For the coconut cream, use the back of a fork to gently crush the creamed coconut into the warm water until dissolved, and the mixture is the consistency of smooth, thick, cream.

10 Zig zag 4 serving plates with the tamarind glaze. Place a rösti in the centre of each plates. Layer paneer and saag on top, finishing with a layer of paneer. Add a spoonful of the coconut cream to the top of each stack. Garnish with small coriander leaves, and finally finish with 1 or 2 edible flowers arranged to one side of each plate.

Autumn vegetable tempura bento box

Tim Anderson ⓜ champion

Preparation time 40 minutes **Cooking time** 1 hout 40 minutes **Serves 4**

Ingredients

For the dashi

20 dried shiitake mushrooms

30cm (12in) square of dried konbu

For the jelly

120ml (4fl oz) umeshu

½ tbsp agar-agar flakes

1 Victoria plum, stoned and quartered

2 tbsp clotted cream

1 tbsp whipping cream

1 tbsp kinako (soybean flour)

1 tsp icing sugar

4 blackberries, to decorate

For the pickles

1 carrot

1 courgette,

12 radishes

salt

100ml (3½fl oz) umezu (ume vinegar)

3 tbsp rice vinegar

3 tbsp prepared dashi

1 tbsp sake

For the roasted romanesco

1 small romanesco, in florets

3 tbsp walnut oil

1 tbsp sansho or Szechuan peppercorns

1 tsp wasabi powder

For the rice

1 tsp chopped fresh ginger,

1 wedge Savoy cabbage

100g (3½oz) Japanese short-grain rice, washed

150ml (5fl oz) prepared dashi

1 tsp hojicha or kukicha tea

3 tbsp pure yuzu juice

5 reserved shiitake mushrooms

8 green shiso leaves, chopped

1 tbsp sesame seeds

For the quail eggs

8 quail eggs

3 tbsp rice vinegar

1 tbsp matcha tea

1 tbsp sencha tea

For the kinpira carrots

2 tbsp vegetable oil

4 carrots, cut into julienne strips

2 red bird's eye chillies, deseeded and cut into julienne strips

2 tbsp soy sauce

1 tbsp mirin

1 tbsp caster sugar

1 tbsp sesame oil

2 tbsp toasted sesame seeds

For the vegetable tempura

½ aubergine, cut into 5mm (¼in) slices

175g (6oz) plain flour

1 egg

250ml (8fl oz) ice cold sparkling water

rapeseed oil, for deep frying

1 small fennel bulb, trimmed and cut into 5mm (¼in) slices

½ butternut squash, peeled, deseeded and cut into 5mm (¼in) slices

4 florets of purple cauliflower

For the sauce

4 tbsp soy sauce

2 tbsp yuzu juice

2 tsp mirin

1 tbsp prepared dashi

Method

1 Make the dashi. Put the mushrooms and konbu into a saucepan with 2 litres (3½ pints) water. Gradually bring to the boil and simmer for 10 minutes. Strain the dashi into a bowl and set aside. Also reserve the mushrooms.

2 For the jelly, gently heat the umeshu and agar-agar flakes in a pan, without stirring, until boiling. Add the quartered plum, bring back to the boil, then simmer for 4 minutes. Spoon into sake cups or small ramekins, leave to cool, then chill in the fridge for around 20 minutes until set. Whisk together the creams, kinako, and icing sugar until light and smooth, then refrigerate until serving.

3 For the pickles, thinly slice the vegetables, preferably on a mandolin. Rub them with a little salt and put into a mixing bowl. Combine the umezu, rice vinegar, 2 tbsp water, the 3 tbsp of prepared dashi, and the sake, and season with salt. Pour over the vegetables and mix gently with your hands. Cover and chill in the fridge until serving, then strain just before using.

Method

4 Preheat the oven to 180°C (350°F/Gas 4). Prepare the roasted romanesco. Toss the romanesco florets in the oil, 2 tsp salt, the sansho, and wasabi powder. Spread out on a baking tray and roast in the oven for 20 minutes until browned and tender. Keep warm until serving.

5 Meanwhile, cook the rice. Blitz the ginger and cabbage in a food processor until minced. Put the cabbage mixture, rice, dashi, tea, and yuzu juice into a saucepan and bring to the boil. As soon as the liquid is boiling, cover the pan with a tight-fitting lid and reduce the heat to the lowest setting. Cook gently for 10 minutes, then remove from the heat and leave to rest, covered, for a further 10 minutes. Chop the shiitake mushrooms. Add to the rice with the shiso, and sesame seeds, and stir to combine. Shape the rice into triangles and keep warm until serving.

6 Boil the quail eggs for 2 minutes in 360ml (12fl oz) water and the rice vinegar. Drain, refresh in cold water, then carefully remove the shells and set the eggs aside. Grind 1 tbsp salt and the teas together with a mortar and pestle until you have a fine powder. Set aside, ready to sift over the eggs just before serving.

7 For the carrots, heat the vegetable oil in a wok or frying pan. Add the carrots and chillies and sauté, stirring, for 2 minutes until the carrots begin to soften. Add the soy sauce, mirin, sugar, and sesame oil and cook for a further 2–3 minutes until glazed and sticky. Mix in the sesame seeds and leave to cool.

8 To make the vegetable tempura, first prepare the aubergine. Sprinkle the aubergine slices with salt, place in a colander, and leave for about 10 minutes to draw the water out. Rinse well under cold water, then pat dry completely on kitchen paper.

9 Make a batter by placing the flour and egg in a bowl. Gradually whisk in the sparkling water until the batter is the consistency of double cream; don't worry if there are a few lumps in the mixture.

10 Heat the rapeseed oil in a deep pan to 180°C (350°F), or until a day-old cube of bread, dropped into the oil, browns in 30 seconds.

11 Dip the prepared aubergine,the sliced fennel and butternut squash, and purple cauliflower florets, a few at a time, in the batter. Shake off excess. Fry in batches in the hot oil for 3–4 minutes until crisp and golden. Drain on kitchen paper. Keep warm.

12 Mix together all the ingredients for the sauce and divide between 4 dipping bowls.

13 To serve, take 8 bento boxes (2 per person). In the first 4 boxes, place the tempura and dipping sauce, the romanesco, and a few pickles. In the second 4 boxes, place the rice, carrots, eggs, pickles, and jelly. To finish, sift some the the ground tea powder over the eggs and top each jelly with the chilled cream and a blackberry to decorate.

Chicken and mushroom "pie"

David Coulson ⓜ Professionals finalist

Preparation time 1 hour 15 minutes   **Cooking time** 3 hours 45 minutes
Serves 4

Ingredients

1 whole chicken

salt and freshly ground black pepper

vegetable oil, for frying and brushing

200ml (7fl oz) chicken stock

150ml (5fl oz) Madeira wine

For the "pies"

4 large flat cap mushrooms

1 celery stick, finely diced

1 carrot, finely diced

1 small leek, finely diced

1 shallot, finely diced

1 garlic clove, crushed

100g (3½oz) wild mushrooms, 4–8 kept whole, the remainder chopped

100ml (3½fl oz) white wine

2–3 tbsp double cream

1 tsp dried chervil

1–2 tsp chopped thyme leaves

100g (3½oz) ready-made puff pastry

plain flour, for dusting

1 egg, beaten

For the creamed potato

500g (1lb 2oz) Maris Piper potatoes, chopped

50g (1¾oz) butter

100ml (3½fl oz) milk

chervil or flat-leaf parsley, to garnish

Method

Method

1 Preheat the oven to 190°C (375°F/Gas 5). Cut off the legs, wings, and breast meat off the chicken. Remove the skin from the breasts and reserve. Wrap the breasts in cling film and twist the ends to secure. Chill for 1 hour, and then poach in simmering water for 20 minutes, or until cooked. Set aside and keep warm.

2 Put the chicken legs into a roasting tin. Season, brush with oil, and roast for 20–30 minutes in the hot oven, or until the meat is cooked. Leave to cool, then remove the skin, cut into strips and reserve. Shred the meat.

3 Remove the tip of the wing joints and cut each wing into 2. Scrape the meat away from the tip of the single-boned pieces. Brown the wings in a little oil in a saucepan. Pour over the stock and Madeira. Bring to the boil, cover, and simmer for 15 minutes. Uncover and reduce the sauce. Remove the wings, set aside and keep warm. Strain the sauce and set aside.

4 Make the "pie" filling. Remove the mushroom stalks, chop, and reserve. Brush mushroom caps with oil and place on a baking tray. Heat a little oil in a pan, add the celery, carrot, leek shallot, garic, chopped wild mushrooms, and the reserved mushroom stalks, and fry until softened. Add the wine, bring to the boil and reduce for about 5 minutes. Stir in the cream, dried chervil, and thyme, and add the shredded leg meat. Season, then pile the mixture onto the mushroom caps on the baking tray.

5 Roll out the pastry on a lightly floured surface. Cut out four 8cm (3in) discs, and place on a greased baking tray and glaze with the beaten egg. Also lay the skin from the chicken breasts on the tray. Place the tray of mushrooms and the tray with the pastry discs and chicken skin in the hot oven for 10–15 minutes until the pastry and the skin are crisp, and the mushrooms softened. Set aside and keep warm.

6 Boil the potatoes in salted water for 10–15 minutes until tender. Drain, roughly mash, then pass though a sieve. Beat in the butter and milk, and keep warm. Fry the reserved whole wild mushrooms in a little oil until softened.

7 To serve, place on a spoonful of the creamed potato on each of 4 plates. Cut each chicken breast in half and put a piece on top of each mound of potato. Place a baked filled mushroom alongside, and put a pastry disc on top to make the "pie". Place 1–2 whole wild mushrooms and a chicken wing on each plate. Reheat the reduced Madeira sauce and drizzle over. Garnish with some of the crispy chicken skin and sprigs of chervil or parsley.

Pan-roasted breast of duck, rainbow chard, carrots, and polenta

John Calton ⓜ **Professionals finalist**

Preparation time 30 minutes   **Cooking time** 45 minutes   **Serves 4**

Ingredients

500g (1lb 2oz) carrots, roughly chopped

1 tbsp extra virgin olive oil, plus extra for dressing

4 duck breasts

200g (7oz) clear honey

200ml (7fl oz) balsamic vinegar

200ml (7fl oz) soy sauce

sprig of rosemary

200g (7oz) chard, plus baby chard to garnish

squeeze of lemon juice

For the polenta

knob of butter

splash of olive oil

1 banana shallot, finely chopped

1 garlic clove

250g (9oz) polenta

about 500ml (16fl oz) carrot juice

100g (3½oz) mascarpone cheese

100g (3½oz) Parmesan cheese, grated

1 bunch each of chives, chervil, and coriander, chopped

salt and freshly ground black pepper

Method →

Method

1 Cook the carrots in boiling water for about 10 minutes or until tender. Transfer to a food processor and blend to a purée. Keep warm.

2 Preheat the oven to 200°C (400°F/Gas 6). Heat the olive oil in a large, heavy frying pan and fry the duck breasts for 7–8 minutes, skin-side down. Transfer to a roasting tin and cook in the hot oven for about 10 minutes to finish. Transfer the duck to a warm plate and leave to rest.

3 Make the polenta. Heat the butter and olive oil in a saucepan and then sweat the shallot and garlic over low heat for about 5 minutes or until soft. Stir in the polenta and then pour on enough carrot juice to cover. Bring to the boil and cook for 5–10 minutes, stirring continuously, until the polenta is soft and the liquid absorbed. Add the

How to make soft and grilled polenta

TECHNIQUE

1 For soft polenta, bring a large pan of salted water to the boil. Gradually pour in the polenta, whisking quickly and continuously to ensure there are no lumps and the mixture is smooth.

2 Reduce the heat to low and continue cooking for 40–45 minutes, or until the polenta is coming away from the sides of the pan, whisking occasionally. Stir in butter, Parmesan cheese, and seasoning.

cheeses, then most of the chopped chives, chervil, and coriander, reserving some for garnishing. Season to taste with salt and pepper.

4 Meanwhile, make a sauce by combining the honey, balsamic vinegar, soy sauce, and rosemary in a saucepan. Bring to the boil and reduce by half. Carefully remove the rosemary.

5 Blanch the chard in boiling water for about 2 minutes. Drain and dress it with olive oil, lemon juice, and seasoning.

6 To serve, cut the duck breasts into slices. Divide the warm polenta between 4 plates. Top with the chard and slices of duck and add spoonfuls of the carrot purée on each side. Pour the sauce around each plate and garnish with the reserved herbs and baby chard.

3 For grilled polenta, make soft polenta, but without butter and cheese. Once thickened, pour it onto a greased baking tray, spread with a spatula, and leave to set. (Keeps for 4 days, covered, in fridge.)

4 When ready to use, turn the chilled polenta out onto a board. Cut into the desired shapes and sizes. Brush pieces with olive oil, then grill on a hot, ridged grill pan for 3–5 minutes on each side.

Fillet of beef with onion purée, mushroom sauce, and fondant potatoes

Nick Pickard ⓜ **Celebrity finalist**

Preparation time 20 minutes   **Cooking time** 1 hour 15 minutes   **Serves 4**

Ingredients

For the fondant potatoes

4 large baking potatoes

200g (7oz) butter, cut in 5–6 slices

3 sprigs of thyme

4 garlic cloves, chopped

For the sauce

500ml (16fl oz) beef stock

100ml (3½fl oz) whipping cream

150g (5½oz) chanterelle mushrooms

25g (scant 1oz) unsalted butter

For the beef

800g (1¾lb) centre-cut beef fillet

olive oil, to coat beef fillet

salt and freshly ground black pepper

For the onion purée

20g (¾oz) unsalted butter

2 tsp olive oil

1 large onion, chopped

3 garlic cloves, chopped

1 tsp chopped thyme

Method

Method

1 Preheat the oven to 180°C (350°F/Gas 4). Peel the potatoes and slice in half down the middle. Trim the rounded side, then cut out a ring of potato from each half using a 6cm (2½in) round cutter so that you have a cylinder of potato.

2 Lay the slices of butter in the bottom of an ovenproof sauté pan. Put the potatoes on top and add water to almost cover the potatoes. Bring to the boil, turn the heat down, and simmer gently for 30 minutes until the potatoes are just tender.

3 Turn the potatoes, add the thyme and garlic, and cook for another 20 minutes. Drain the potatoes and keep warm.

4 For the sauce, pour the stock into a pan, boil to reduce by two-thirds, then whisk in the cream. Fry the mushrooms in the butter for 5 minutes until golden brown, then add to the stock and cream. Season to taste and set aside. Reheat gently before serving.

5 Rub the beef all over with the olive oil and season generously. Heat a large ovenproof frying pan until smoking, then add the beef and sear for 2 minutes on each side until golden brown. Transfer to the hot oven and roast for 15–20 minutes until cooked to your liking, then remove from the oven and rest for 15 minutes.

6 Meanwhile, make the onion purée. Heat the butter and oil in a pan. Add the onion, garlic, and thyme. Cook gently for 15 minutes until completely soft but not brown. Cool slightly. Purée in a blender until smooth. Return to the pan and season. Reheat gently before serving.

7 Spread a little warm onion purée on each of 4 serving plates. Carve the beef into 4 thick slices and place a slice on each plate, on top of the purée. Put 2 fondant potatoes on each plate, pour on some of the reheated mushroom sauce, and serve.

Beef wrapped in coppa di Parma with Swiss chard and soft polenta

Neil Stuke @ Celebrity semi-finalist

Preparation time 20 minutes   **Cooking time** 40 minutes   **Serves 4**

Ingredients

1kg (2¼lb) beef fillet

100g (3½oz) fat from prosciutto di Parma

2 garlic cloves, finely sliced

1 sprig of rosemary, leaves and stalks separated

sea salt and freshly ground black pepper

10 thin slices coppa di Parma

2 tbsp olive oil

2 celery sticks, chopped

1 red onion, chopped

2 sprigs of thyme

1 bay leaf

360ml (12fl oz) full-bodied red wine such as Barolo

200ml (7fl oz) beef stock

30g (1oz) butter

200g (7oz) polenta

For the chard

450g (1lb) Swiss chard, stalks removed

2 tbsp olive oil

2 garlic cloves, finely chopped

1 dried chilli, crushed

Method →

Method

1 With a sharp knife, make small incisions all over the beef, following the grain of the meat, and insert a sliver of prosciutto fat, a slice of garlic, and some rosemary leaves. Season with salt and pepper.

2 Wrap the fillet in the coppa di Parma, and tie evenly with string. Heat the oil in a deep sauté pan and sear the beef on all sides. Remove the beef.

3 Add the celery and onion to the pan and sauté, stirring, for 5 minutes, until softened. Stir in the thyme, bay leaf, and rosemary stalks. Pour in the wine and beef stock, bring to the boil, and return the beef to the pan. Place some damp greaseproof paper over the pan, and then cover with the lid. Simmer for 20–30 minutes. Lift out the beef, transfer to a warm plate, and leave to rest.

4 Strain the cooking juices into a clean pan, discard the vegetables, and simmer the liquid until it has reduced by half. Season with salt and pepper, stir in 15g (½oz) butter, and keep hot.

5 To prepare the polenta, cook in a pan of boiling water as directed on the packet to end up with a soft consistency. Add the remaining butter and season well with salt and pepper to taste.

6 For the Swiss chard, blanch the leaves in a saucepan of boiling salted water for about 2–3 minutes, and drain well. Heat the oil in a frying pan, add the garlic and chilli and cook for 1–2 minutes, stirring. Add the chard and stir-fry quickly for 2 minutes.

7 To serve, remove the string and slice the beef fillet into thick slices. Spoon the polenta, just off centre, into 4 large serving bowls, and place the Swiss chard on top. Rest a thick slice of the beef on top, then spoon some hot sauce over it and around the bowl.

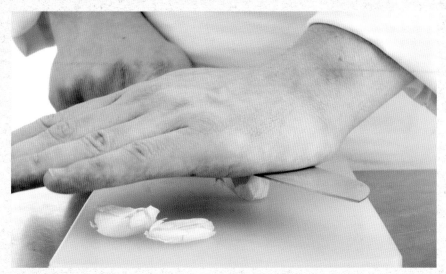

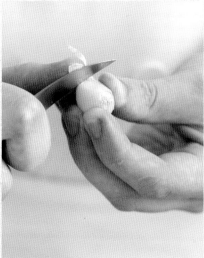

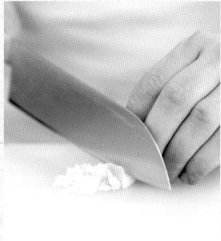

How to chop garlic

Place each garlic clove on a cutting board. Cover with the flat side of a large knife and pound with the palm of your hand. Pushing down on the cloves should make it easier to peel away the papery skin. Discard this, then cut off ends of each clove. Slice clove into slivers lengthways, then cut across into tiny chunks. Pile up the pieces and chop again for finer pieces.

Loin of venison with celeriac purée, braised cabbage, and redcurrant jus

Alex Rushmer @ finalist

Preparation time 20 minutes   **Cooking time** 1 hour 30 minutes   **Serves 4**

Ingredients

750g (1lb 10oz) loin of venison

1 tbsp olive oil

knob of butter

100g (3½oz) porcini or wild mushrooms, cut into thick slices

For the cabbage

knob of butter

1 small shallot, diced

300g (10oz) red cabbage, quartered, cored, and sliced

1 apple, cored, peeled, and sliced

1 tbsp clear honey

3 tbsp red wine vinegar

100ml (3½fl oz) red wine

200ml (7fl oz) chicken stock

salt and freshly ground black pepper

For the celeriac

1 celeriac, approx. 800g (1¾lb)

juice of 1 lemon

3 tbsp double cream

25g (scant 1oz) butter

500ml (16fl oz) vegetable oil

For the jus

knob of butter

1 shallot, diced

8 juniper berries

50g (1¾oz) redcurrants

150ml (5fl oz) port

150ml (5fl oz) veal stock

2 tsp redcurrant jelly

Method

Method

1 For the cabbage, melt the butter in a large heavy saucepan. Add the shallot and cook for about 5 minutes to soften. Add the remaining ingredients and season. Cover with greaseproof paper and a lid and braise over very low heat for 1½ hours, stirring occasionally.

2 Peel the celeriac. Shave off 4 strips to make crisps, and put in a bowl of iced lemon water and set aside. Dice the rest. Put in a pan with water to cover, salt, and lemon juice and bring to the boil. Simmer for 15–20 minutes, or until soft. Drain and transfer to a blender or food processor. Add the cream, butter, and seasoning and purée. Keep warm.

3 For the jus, melt the butter in a pan. Cook the shallot for 3 minutes to soften. Add the juniper berries and redcurrants, and cook for 1 minute, then stir in the port and reduce by half. Pour in the veal stock and reduce again. Stir in the redcurrant jelly and pass through a sieve into a clean pan. Keep warm.

4 Season the venison and fry in the olive oil for 10–15 minutes, turning once. Cook longer if you prefer your meat less pink. Remove the venison from the pan, leave to rest, and then slice. Add the butter and mushrooms to the pan and fry for about 2 minutes to cook through.

5 Just before serving, drain and dry the celeriac shavings. Deep-fry in the vegetable oil for 2–3 minutes until crisp. Drain on kitchen paper.

6 Spoon the purée and cabbage onto 4 warm serving plates. Top the purée with slices of venison and the cabbage with mushrooms. Drizzle over the warm jus, and garnish each plate with a celeriac crisp.

Sheer
Indulgence

Spiced battered fish and chips

Dhruv Baker Ⓜ champion

Preparation time 40 minutes   **Cooking time** 50 minutes   **Serves 4**

Ingredients

4 John Dory fillets, or other white fish, approx. 150g (5½oz) each

handful of coriander, roughly chopped, to garnish

For the mushy peas

250g (9oz) dried split green or yellow peas

2 onions, chopped

2 bay leaves

salt and freshly ground black pepper

handful of coriander, chopped

1–2 red chillies, deseeded and chopped

1–2 green chillies, deseeded and chopped

juice of 2–3 limes

300g (10oz) frozen or fresh peas

For the brown sauce

2 tbsp tamarind paste

4 tsp caster sugar

juice of 2 limes

pinch of chilli powder

For the batter

150g (5½oz) plain flour

2 tsp baking powder

½ tsp fennel seeds

¼ tsp turmeric

¼ tsp chilli powder

¼ tsp ground coriander

¼ tsp ground cumin

¼ tsp brown mustard seeds

½ tsp ginger paste, or freshly grated root ginger

½ tsp garlic paste, or 1 garlic clove, finely crushed

For the chips

4–6 large Maris Piper potatoes, peeled and cut into chips

groundnut oil, for deep-frying

Method

Method

1 Put the dried peas in a saucepan with 1 litre (1¾ pints) of water, the onions, bay leaves, and some black pepper. Boil for 1¼ hours or until the peas are tender and mushy, adding more water if necessary. Add the coriander, chillies, and lime juice. In another pan, boil the frozen or fresh peas for 4–5 minutes or until just tender, then drain and crush, using a fork. Stir into the split peas and season with salt.

2 For the sauce, put the tamarind paste in a small pan with the sugar, lime juice, and 4 tbsp of water. Add the chilli powder. Boil over medium-high heat for 5 minutes or until reduced to a sticky sauce.

How to batter and fry fish

TECHNIQUE

1 Mix the batter according to your recipe instructions, and leave to stand for 30 minutes. Put 2 tbsp seasoned flour in a dish and coat the fish with it.

2 Beat egg white in a metal bowl until stiff peaks form. Gently fold the whisked egg white into the batter, using a wooden spoon, until combined.

3 Parboil the chips in a pan of boiling water for 5 minutes, then drain. Heat a deep-fat fryer or deep pan, two-thirds full of oil, to 160°C (325°F). Fry the chips in batches for 5–6 minutes, then drain on kitchen paper. Increase the temperature of the oil to 180°C (350°F), return the chips to the pan until crisp and golden. Toss in salt.

4 For the batter, mix the flour, baking powder, spices, ginger, and garlic with 150–175ml (5–6fl oz) iced water until smooth. Dip 2 pieces of fish in the batter and deep fry for 7–8 minutes, turning once or twice. Drain and set aside to keep warm, then repeat with the remaining fish.

5 Serve the battered fish with the chips and mushy peas alongside. Drizzle a little brown sauce over and garnish the plates with coriander.

3 Using a 2-pronged fork, dip a piece of floured fish in the batter, turning to coat. Lift out fish and hold it over the bowl for 5 seconds so excess batter can drip off.

4 Heat enough oil for deep-frying to 180°C (350°F). Carefully lower the fish, 1 or 2 pieces at a time into the oil and deep-fry, turning once, for 6–8 minutes, or until golden brown and crisp.

Monkfish with butternut squash fondant and sauce vierge

Lisa Faulkner @ Celebrity champion

Preparation time 35 minutes   **Cooking time** 30 minutes   **Serves 4**

Ingredients

50g (1¾oz) butter

300g (10oz) butternut squash, cut into rounds approx. 1.5cm (½in) thick

150ml (5fl oz) fish stock

salt and freshly ground black pepper

175g (6oz) French beans

4 slices wafer-thin pancetta

4 monkfish fillets, approx. 200g (7oz) each, skinned and cut into medallions approx. 2.5cm (1in) thick

1 tbsp olive oil

sprigs of basil, to garnish

For the sauce vierge

3 tomatoes on the vine, skinned, deseeded and finely diced

1 garlic clove, finely chopped

2 tbsp tarragon, chopped

2 tbsp basil, chopped

100ml (3½fl oz) olive oil, plus extra

2 tsp lemon juice

Method

1 Preheat the oven to 200°C (400°F/Gas 6). Melt the butter in an ovenproof frying pan, large enough to accomodate the butternut squash. Add the squash, and cook over a high heat for 2 minutes on each side. Add the stock, season with salt and pepper, and cook in the oven for 20–25 minutes, or until tender. Leave oven on.

2 For the sauce vierge, mix the tomatoes with the garlic and herbs, then moisten with olive oil and lemon juice. Season well.

3 Blanch the French beans in a pan of boiling salted water for 3–4 minutes. Drain and refresh under cold running water. Pat dry, then separate into 4 ittle bundles and wrap each with a slice of pancetta. Secure with a cocktail stick. Place on a baking tray and put in the hot oven for about 5 minutes, or until the beans are heated through and the pancetta is crispy.

4 Brush the monkfish with olive oil and season well. Heat a non-stick frying pan and cook the fish for 3–4 minutes each side, or until cooked through.

5 Put some butternut squash on 4 serving plates, arrange the monkfish around it and spoon the sauce vierge over and around. Place a bundle of beans on one side. Garnish with basil.

TECHNIQUE

How to skin fish fillets

1 Place fillet skin-side down on a board. Using a long, sharp knife, make an incision near the tail end, tilting the blade at an angle. Carefully cut into the flesh just to, but not through, the skin.

2 Angle the knife until blade is almost flat, and with your other hand, firmly grasp the end of the skin. Keep the knife as close to the skin as possible as you cut, and slowly pull the skin away.

Roasted crown of lamb with minted pea purée

Christopher Souto @ semi-finalist

Preparation time 30 minutes   **Cooking time** 30 minutes   **Serves 4**

Ingredients

8 Charlotte potatoes

4 tbsp olive oil

2 garlic cloves

2 racks of lamb (6 ribs each), French-trimmed

salt and freshly ground black pepper

200g (7oz) frozen peas

4 sprigs of mint

1 tsp red wine vinegar

200ml (7fl oz) chicken stock

2 tbsp melted butter

3 sprigs of rosemary

300ml (10fl oz) red wine

Method

1 Preheat oven to 200°C (400°F/Gas 6). Boil potatoes with their skins on in salted water for 15–20 minutes until almost cooked. Drain and peel. Cut into cylinders with a 2cm (¾in) pastry cutter, then slice into 1cm (½in) thick discs.

2 Heat half the oil in a frying pan over high heat. Halve garlic cloves and rub over the lamb (keep garlic cloves for the potatoes). Season lamb with salt and pepper, then sear in the hot oil until browned on all sides. Put in a roasting tin in the oven for 18–20 minutes. Leave to rest.

3 Meanwhile, cook the peas in salted boiling water for about 3 minutes. Drain and purée in a blender with the mint leaves and vinegar, adding some chicken stock to achieve the required consistency. Season with salt and pepper and keep warm.

4 Heat butter and remaining oil over a medium heat, together with 2 sprigs of the rosemary and the reserved garlic. Cook the potato discs until golden on both sides. Remove the rosemary and garlic and season to taste.

5 Heat the wine in a pan with the remaining rosemary and reduce by two-thirds. Add the rest of the chicken stock and reduce by half. Season the sauce and remove the rosemary.

6 To serve, carve the lamb into cutlets and place 3 on each of 4 serving plates. Add some pea purée and potatoes. Drizzle the sauce over the lamb and serve.

Quail parcels of chicken liver with onion soubise and spinach and pear purée

Steven Wallis @ champion

Preparation time 30 minutes   **Cooking time** 35 minutes   **Serves 4**

4 boned quails (ask your butcher to bone them), at room temperature

salt and freshly ground black pepper

a few sprigs of thyme, leaves only

4 large chicken livers

2 tbsp olive oil

60ml (2fl oz) Cognac

100ml (3½fl oz) port or red wine

200ml (7fl oz) chicken stock

60g (2oz) butter

For the soubise

500g (1lb 2oz) onions, finely sliced

40g (1¼oz) salted butter

3 tbsp olive oil

freshly ground white pepper

For the purée

500g (1lb 2oz) mature spinach leaves

20g (¾oz) salted butter

2 large Comice pears, peeled and cored

½ tsp grated nutmeg

Method

1 First prepare the soubise. Place the onions in a pan with the butter, olive oil, a pinch of salt, and a few grinds of white pepper. Cut a cover made from greaseproof paper to fit over the onions and cook over a very low heat for 20–30 minutes,until they are soft but not browned. Purée in a food processor, return to the pan, and keep warm.

2 Preheat the oven to 200°C (400°F/Gas 6). Open out the boned quails, and place skin-side down on a work surface, season with salt and black pepper, and scatter over the thyme leaves. In a small pan, flash fry the chicken livers in 1 tbsp of oil for a few seconds, stir in the Cognac, and continue cooking to burn off the alcohol. Remove livers from the heat and season well.

3 Spread the cooked livers over the opened-out quails, wrap the quails around the livers to form tight parcels, and secure the parcels with wooden cocktail sticks. In the same pan as the livers were cooked, flash fry the quail parcels for a few minutes unitl browned all over. Place on a baking tray and cook in the hot oven for 15 minutes, until the quail juices just run clear when the breast meat is stabbed with a skewer. Cover with foil and leave to rest for 5 minutes.

4 Meanwhile, reheat the pan in which you cooked the livers and quails and deglaze with port. Add the chicken stock and reduce until syrupy, then whisk in the butter. Set aside and keep warm

5 For the purée, wilt the spinach in a pan with the butter, squeeze out as much water as possible and set aside. Poach the pears in water for about 15 minutes, or until soft. Drain and then put into a food processor, along with the spinach, nutmeg, and some seasoning. Blitz to a fine purée.

6 To serve, place 1 tbsp of soubise on each of 4 serving plates, tapering it into an elegant sweep across the plate. Remove the cocktail sticks from the quail parcels and place, crown side up with the wings and legs tucked in, on top. Add quenelles of the pear and spinach purée on one side, and then spoon over the port wine jus.

Duck breast with buttered baby turnips and duck jus

Steven Wallis @ champion

Preparation time 1 hour   **Cooking time** 1 hour 30 minutes   **Serves 4**

Ingredients

70cl bottle Pinot Noir

300ml (10fl oz) Madeira wine

1 duck carcass, as much fat removed as possible

2 litres (3½ pints) chicken stock

1 carrot, finely diced

1 leek, finely diced

1 celery stick, finely diced

2 banana shallots, diced

bouquet garni of bay leaf, thyme sprig, few parsley stalks, and star anise

25g (scant 1oz) unsalted butter

pinch of finely chopped rosemary

For the vegetables

1 leek, white parts only, sliced into julienne strips

100ml (3½fl oz) whole milk

about 45g (1½oz) rice flour

8–10 baby turnips, depending on size

500ml (16fl oz) chicken stock

handful of Swiss chard leaves, torn

vegetable oil, for deep frying

knob of unsalted butter, melted

For the potatoes

225g (8oz) small waxy potatoes

60g (2oz) oak chips, for smoking

drizzle of extra virgin olive oil

2 tsp snipped fresh chives

salt and freshly ground black pepper

For the duck breasts

2 large duck breasts, skin scored

pinch of fleur de sel or other sea salt

Method

1 Preheat the oven to 220°C (425°F/Gas 7). Pour both wines into a heavy pan, and simmer to reduce by a third. Meanwhile, roast the duck carcass in the oven for 20 minutes. Place carcass in a large pan and add the stock, vegetables, and bouquet garni. Bring to the boil and skim off any froth. Add the wine and simmer until the liquid is reduced by half. Strain through a fine sieve. Pour half into a clean pan (freeze the rest for another recipe), and reduce again by half.

2 Prepare the vegetables. Soak leeks in the milk for 10 minutes. Drain and coat in flour. Poach turnips in the chicken stock for 20 minutes until tender, lift out and keep warm. Blanch chard in the stock for 5 minutes until tender. Heat the oil in a deep pan and fry the leek strips until crisp. Drain on kitchen paper. Boil potatoes in salted water for 15–20 minutes until tender. Drain, return to pan, cover with cling film, and leave until the skins will slide off easily. Smoke by heating over oak chips and set aside.

3 Place the duck breasts in a cold frying pan, skin-side down. Cook over medium heat for 10 minutes, or until the skin is crisp. Turn over and cook for 5 minutes. Leave to rest.

4 Crush the potatoes in a small pan with a drizzle of olive oil. Stir in the chives, season with salt and black pepper and keep warm. Make a jus by reheating the reduced duck stock until bubbling. Whisk in the butter, add the rosemary, taste and adjust the seasoning.

5 Spoon potatoes onto 4 warm plates and top with Swiss chard. Slice duck, sprinkle with fleur de sel and place on the chard. Arrange the turnips around the plate and glaze with melted butter and chicken stock. Spoon over some jus and finish with a neat pile of leek crisps on top.

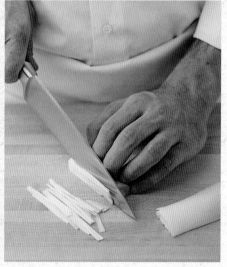

How to cut leeks julienne

With a sharp knife, trim off the root end and some of the dark, green top. Cut leek in half lengthways and spread layers apart. Rinse under cold running water to remove the soil that tends to collect between the layers, then pat dry with kitchen paper. Lay the halved leek flat-side down on the chopping board and slice it into thick or thin strips, according to your recipe.

Roasted pigeon with pommes mousseline and pancetta peas

Claire Lara @ Professionals champion

Preparation time 30 minutes   **Cooking time** 1 hour   **Serves 4**

Ingredients

4 pigeons

225g (8oz) butter, softened

250g (9oz) duck fat

4 Rooster potatoes

salt and freshly ground black pepper

200ml (7fl oz) double cream, warmed

1 tbsp olive oil

1 garlic clove, crushed

1 sprig of thyme

100g (3½oz) pancetta

175g (6oz) shelled fresh peas

300ml (10fl oz) game stock

200g (7oz) quince jelly, finely diced

2 Baby Gem lettuce, finely shredded

½ bunch of flat-leaf parsley

Method

1 Preheat the oven to 130°C (250°F/Gas 1) and remove the wishbone from the pigeons. Heat 75g (2½oz) of the butter in a heavy saucepan, add the pigeons, and brown them by turning the birds quickly in the hot butter. Remove the pigeons from the pan, leave to cool a little, then remove the legs. Reserve the butter.

2 Place the legs in an ovenproof dish with a close fitting lid, melt the duck fat and pour it over the legs. Cover and cook in the hot oven for about 45 minutes or until tender, turning the legs over once. Remove from the oven and increase the temperature to 220°C (425°F/Gas 7).

3 To make the pommes mousseline, cook the potatoes in a saucepan of lightly salted simmering water for about 20 minutes or until soft. Drain and skin the potatoes when they are cool enough to handle. Put them through a vegetable mouli and gradually beat in 150g (5½oz) of the butter and all the warmed cream. The potato purée should be very smooth and shiny. Season to taste. Keep warm.

4 For the pancetta peas, heat the oil in a heavy saucepan. Add the garlic, thyme, and pancetta and cook over medium heat for about 10 minutes or until the pancetta is crispy. Set aside. Drain off excess fat and remove the thyme. Simmer the peas gently in salted water for 10`minutes until just tender. Drain and set aside.

5 Make a sauce by pouring the stock into a pan. Add the quince jelly and boil until reduced by about half and is richly coloured and syrupy.

6 Put the pigeons in a roasting tin, season with salt and pepper, and brush with the butter used in step 1. Roast in the oven for 15 minutes, basting once. Leave to rest. Remove the meat from the cooked legs.

7 Add the peas and lettuce to the browned pancetta with 2 tbsp of sauce. Heat gently until the lettuce has wilted slightly.

8 To serve, carve the pigeon breasts and lay with some of the leg meat on a mound of pommes mousseline in 4 serving bowls. Scatter around the pea, lettuce and pancetta mixture, pour on sauce, and garnish with parsley.

Salmon en papillotte with braised fennel and a creamy caper sauce

Chris Gates ⓜ **finalist**

Preparation time 15 minutes   **Cooking time** 35 minutes   **Serves 4**

Ingredients

4 salmon fillets, 200g (7oz) each, skin removed

1 fennel bulb, sliced

1 lemon, sliced

60g (2oz) butter

about 120ml (4fl oz) white wine

salt and freshly ground black pepper

1 shallot, finely chopped

1 tbsp capers, drained

200ml (7fl oz) double cream

1 tbsp fresh chopped dill

Method

1 Preheat the oven to 190°C (375°F/Gas 5). Fold 4 sheets of baking parchment in half and fold over 2 of the edges twice, leaving the remaining edge open to make a bag.

2 Place a salmon fillet in each bag with 2 slices of fennel, 2 slices of lemon, a knob of the butter, and 2 tbsp white wine. Season with salt and pepper. Close the bags by folding the baking parchment over twice on the remaining side. Place bags on a baking tray and cook in the hot oven for about 20 minutes until the fish is ready – it should be paler in colour and just set.

3 Make a sauce by softening the shallot in the remaining butter for 10 minutes until translucent. Add the capers and cream and simmer gently for 5 minutes until the sauce has thickened. Season and stir in the dill just before serving.

4 Once the fish is just cooked, cut open the bags and place a salmon fillet onto each of 4 warmed serving plates. Spoon over the fennel and juices left in the bag, discarding the lemon. Drizzle some of the caper sauce around the salmon and serve.

Bringing umami out of chaos

Tim Anderson Ⓜ champion

Preparation time 1 hour   **Cooking time** 3 hours   **Serves 4**

For the dashi

20cm (8in) dried konbu seaweed

10 dried shiitake mushrooms

1 litre (1¾ pints) soft mineral water (or softened tap water)

50g (1¾oz) katsuobushi flakes

For the pork belly

500g (1lb 2oz) pork belly, rind removed

450ml (15fl oz) cola

300ml (10fl oz) prepared dashi

150ml (5fl oz) shoyu

150ml (5fl oz) Worcestershire sauce

5 tbsp red wine

5 tbsp mirin

2 star anise

1½ tsp Marmite

For the celery

1 celery stick, halved widthways

100g (3½oz) caster sugar

3 tbsp water

1 tsp yuzu juice

For the fondant squash

1 small red kuri squash, approx.12cm (5in) in diameter, washed

2 tbsp olive oil

100g (3½oz) butter

100ml (3½fl oz) dashi

100ml (3½fl oz) red wine

For the roasted turnips

16 baby turnips

2 tbsp walnut oil

salt and white pepper

For the peas

250ml (8fl oz) prepared dashi

2 tbsp shelled peas

For the miso mustard

30g (1oz) white miso

30g (1oz) Dijon mustard

3 tbsp dry white vermouth

100ml (3½oz) prepared dashi

1 egg yolk

2 tbsp walnut oil

30g (1oz) parmesan cheese, grated

For the dashi pearls

100ml (3½oz) prepared dashi

2 tsp shoyu

2 tsp mirin

1 tsp yuzu juice

2.5g sodium alginate

7.5g calcium chloride powder

120ml (4fl oz) soft water

To garnish

handful of shiso cress

handful of salad cress

Method

1 To make the dashi, steep the konbu seaweed and shitake mushrooms in the water for 15–20 minutes until soft. Heat the water very gently, removing the mushrooms before it boils. Once it boils, reduce to a simmer and cook the konbu for 10 minutes, then remove. Add the katsuobushi flakes, strain the liquid once they sink, and set aside.

2 For the cola-roasted pork belly, preheat the oven to 160°C (325°F/Gas 3). Place the pork in a roasting tin. Whisk together the remaining ingredients and pour them over the pork. Roast in the hot oven for 2 hours, basting frequently. Remove the pork from the oven and rest for 15 minutes. Carve into 4 neat rectangular pieces. Leave oven on. Meanwhile, prepare the celery. Cut 4 strips of celery, no thicker than 3mm (⅛in) each, and trim into a neat, rectangular shape. Dissolve the sugar in the water and yuzu juice and bring to the boil. Allow sugar to caramelize to a light amber colour, then add the celery and remove the pan from the heat. Leave the celery to cook in the hot syrup for 4 minutes, then drain and cool on greaseproof paper, brushing off the excess syrup with a wet pastry brush.

3 Slice the squash vertically into 4 rings, each around 2cm (¾in) thick, and scoop out the seeds. Melt the oil and butter in an ovenproof frying pan and cook the squash rings on one side for about 4 minutes until nicely browned. Turn them over and add enough dashi and wine to come just below the top of the squash. Transfer to the oven and cook for about 30 minutes, until the squash is very soft and most of the liquid has evaporated. Set aside and keep warm.

4 Toss the turnips with the oil, salt, and pepper. Place in a roasting tray and roast in the hot oven for 45 minutes.

5 Meanwhile, to cook the peas, bring the dashi to the boil in a saucepan and blanch the peas in it until they are just tender. When cool enough to handle, remove their outer skin.

6 To cook the miso mustard, whisk together the miso, mustard, vermouth, dashi, and egg yolk in a bain-marie or a bowl set over a pan of simmering water. Slowly drizzle in the oil, whisking constantly until emulsified. Whisk in the Parmesan cheese and keep warm.

7 To make the dashi pearls, ensure that the dashi is cool. Using a blender, mix together the dashi, shoyu, mirin, yuzu juice, and sodium alginate until completely homogenous. Allow the air bubbles to dissipate. Stir the calcium chloride into the soft water until completely dissolved. With a pipette, drop the dashi mixture into the calcium chloride bath and leave to set for 45 seconds, then remove with a small slotted spoon and rinse under cold water. Just before serving, combine with the peas.

8 To serve, set a squash ring in the middle of each of 4 serving plates and pour a small pool of the braising liquid in the centre. Place a piece of pork on top and balance some celery on the pork. Arrange roasted turnips around the squash and spoon some mustard miso around the rim of the plates. Decorate with the peas and dashi pearls, and finish by garnishing with the shiso and salad cress.

Gnudi

John Torode ⓜ judge

Preparation time 20 minutes **Cooking time** 2 hours 30 minutes **Serves 4**

Ingredients

For the dumplings

250g (9oz) fine semolina flour

250g (9oz) ricotta cheese

50g (1¾oz) Parmesan cheese, finely grated

For the beef stew

750g (1lb 10oz) shin or skirt of beef or ox cheek, cut into bite-sized chunks

salt and freshly ground black pepper

4 tbsp olive oil

200g (7oz) thick bacon, cut into big chunks

2 carrots, halved and cut in half lengthways

2 leeks, cut into strips the same size as the carrots

2 celery sticks, cut into strips the same size as the carrots

2 x 400g cans chopped tomatoes

2 bay leaves

small bunch of flat-leaf parsley

small bunch of sage

360ml (12fl oz) red wine

To serve

handful of parsley, chopped

Parmesan cheese, grated

Method →

Method

1 About 24 hours ahead of cooking the dish, prepare the dumplings. Coat a flat tray with a layer of the semolina flour. Mix the ricotta with a fork and add the Parmesan cheese. Roll into a long log and then break off pieces and shape them into dessert spoon-size balls. Roll each ball in semolina flour and place on the tray so they do not touch. Pour the remaining the semolina over, so that the balls are almost completely covered. Place in the fridge, uncovered, and leave overnight.

2 When you are ready to cook the dish, preheat the oven to 190ºC (375°F/Gas 5).

3 To make the stew, season the meat well, and heat the oil in a large flameproof casserole dish. Add the bacon, cook it for 2 minutes, then add the meat. Leave it to sit and sizzle until the chunks are well browned underneath, when they will naturally lift and come away from the pan. Turn them over and cook for a further 10 minutes, making sure to move the bacon so it does not burn. You can always take the bacon out and return it to the sauce at the next step.

4 Add the vegetables and pour in the tomatoes. Add the bay leaves, parsley, and sage and season well with salt and pepper. Then add the wine and bring to the boil, increasing the heat so the alcohol evaporates. Let it bubble for about 10 minutes, scraping the sticky bits of meat from the bottom of the pot.

5 Add about 500ml (16fl oz) of water, so that it almost covers the meat. Cover the casserole and place in the hot oven for 1 hour, then take the lid off, give the meat a good stir, and reduce the oven temperature to 160°C (325°F/Gas 3). Cook the stew uncovered for another hour, so that a lot of the liquid evaporates.

6 Leave the stew to cool for about 30 minutes, then, using two forks, pull the meat apart and shred it well. If the stew is too thin, return it to the boil and reduce, but remember this will be served with pasta or bread so it should not be dry. Discard the herbs and check and adjust the seasoning, if needed. Set aside and keep warm.

7 To cook the dumplings, bring a large saucepan of water to the boil with a good amount of salt. Dust off the excess semolina flour and drop the dumplings into the water. Let them float to the top and cook for 3 minutes. Then, using a slotted spoon, drop them into the stew and gently stir. Stir in the chopped parsley.

8 Spoon the stew and dumplings into 4 warm serving bowls. Top with Parmesan, and serve with chunks of bread or freshly cooked pasta.

Fillet steak with beetroot rösti and red wine jus

Cheryl Avery Ⓜ quarter-finalist

Preparation time 25 minutes   **Cooking time** 45minutes   **Serves 4**

Ingredients

4 fillets of beef steak, about 150g (5½oz) each

1 tbsp olive oil

50g (1¾oz) curly kale

For the red wine jus

4 garlic cloves

1 tbsp olive oil

100ml (3½fl oz) red wine

100ml (3½fl oz) beef stock

For the beetroot röstis

2 beetroot, peeled and grated

2 large potatoes, about 200g (7oz) each, peeled and coarsely grated

1 small onion, coarsely grated

salt and freshly ground black pepper

1 large egg, beaten

1–2 tbsp vegetable oil

Method

Method

1 Preheat the oven to 190°C (375°F/Gas 5). For the jus, toss the garlic cloves in the olive oil, then roast on a small baking tray in the hot oven for 15–20 minutes until very soft. Set aside.

2 Meanwhile, to make the röstis, mix together the beetroot and potato, then squeeze out any excess liquid. Stir in the onion and season with salt and pepper. Add enough of the egg to bind everything, then shape into 4 thin rounds.

3 Heat a large, ovenproof frying pan until hot then pour in the oil. Add the röstis and fry for 4–5 minutes on each side or until crisp and golden. Transfer to the hot oven for 6–8 minutes or until cooked through. Keep warm.

4 To cook the steaks, heat a frying pan until hot. Rub the steaks with a little olive oil and season. Put the steaks in the hot pan and fry for 2½–3 minutes on each side for a medium-rare finish. Remove from the pan and leave to rest.

5 Put the kale in a steamer over a pan of boiling water. Steam gently for 4–5 minutes or until tender. Season, set aside and keep warm.

6 To finish the jus, pour the red wine into the frying pan that the steak was cooked in. Stir in well to deglaze the pan. Squeeze the flesh from the roasted garlic, mash until smooth and add to the pan. Then stir in the beef stock and simmer for 1–2 minutes to reduce slightly.

7 To serve, place a rösti on each of 4 serving plates, top with some kale, and then a steak, Drizzle jus over the steak and around the plate.

1 Heat the grill pan (alternatively a grill or a barbecue) over a high heat. Brush both sides of the steak with oil, and season to taste with salt and freshly ground black pepper.

2 When the pan is very hot, place the steaks diagonally across the ridges. Cook for half the desired time, (turning 45 degrees to create a diamond pattern), then turn the steaks over. Remove and allow to rest.

3 For a very rare steak, cook the meat for about 2–3 minutes, until just seared, on both sides. The steak should feel very soft when pressed, and the interior should be reddish purple when the meat is sliced.

4 For a rare steak, cook the meat for a total of 6–8 minutes, turning over at the point where drops of blood start to come to the surface. It should feel soft and spongy, and the interior should be red.

5 For a medium-rare steak, cook for a total of 8–10 minutes, but turn the meat when drops of juice are first visible. The steak should offer resistance when pressed, and be pink in the centre.

6 A well done steak needs to be cooked for a total of 12–14 minutes. Turn the meat when drops of juice are clearly visible. The steak should feel firm and be brown throughout.

Beef Wellington with mash, creamed Savoy cabbage, and an oxtail jus

Liz McClarnon @ **Celebrity champion**

Preparation time 40 minutes   **Cooking time** 1 hour   **Serves 4**

Ingredients

3 Maris Piper potatoes, peeled and chopped

4 large stoneless prunes

4 tsp mango chutney

2 streaky bacon rashers, cut in half

250g (9oz) ready-made puff pastry

splash of milk

200g (7oz) chestnut mushrooms, chopped

75g (2½oz) salted butter

salt and freshly ground black pepper

2 tsp truffle oil

½ Savoy cabbage, shredded

400ml (14fl oz) double cream

4 beef fillets, about 175g (6oz) each

1 tbsp olive oil

3 sprigs of thyme

2 sprigs of rosemary

For the oxtail jus

2 garlic cloves, chopped

1 shallot, chopped

1 tbsp olive oil

3 sprigs of flat-leaf parsley, chopped

300ml (10fl oz) port

200ml (7fl oz) oxtail stock, plus 4 tbsp

Method

1 Preheat oven to 200°C (400°F/Gas 6). Simmer the potatoes in salted water for 20 minutes, or until cooked. Drain and keep warm.

2 For the jus, put the garlic and shallot in a frying pan with the oil and parsley. Add port, bring to the boil and reduce by three-quarters. Add the stock and reduce by half. Keep warm.

3 Fill the hole in each prune with the chutney and roll in a piece of streaky bacon. Pierce with a cocktail stick and cook on a baking tray in the hot oven for 7 minutes. Remove from the oven and keep warm. Leave the oven on.

4 Roll out the pastry and cut out four 8cm (3in) diameter circles. Put them on a floured baking sheet, glaze with a little milk, then cook in the hot oven for 12 minutes, until golden. Remove and keep warm.

5 Meanwhile, cook the mushrooms in 25g (scant 1oz) of the butter in a saucepan, add seasoning and the truffle oil. Keep warm.

6 Put the cabbage in 300ml (10fl oz) of the double cream in a saucepan, and add seasoning. Cook for 10–12 minutes until tender.

7 Mash the potatoes with the rest of the double cream and butter. Set aside and keep warm.

8 Cover the beef in the olive oil and salt and pepper. Heat a frying pan and when hot seal the beef for a few seconds on each side. Transfer to a roasting tin, add the thyme and rosemary and spoon the extra 4 tbsp stock over the top. Put in the hot oven for 6 minutes.

9 To serve, place a puff pastry circle on each of 4 plates. Score a circle in the top, push it down, and fill with warm mushrooms. Place a fillet of beef on top. Put some creamed cabbage, a prune in bacon, and quenelles of mash alongside. then drizzle over the jus.

Beef fillet with trompettes noires, celeriac, and potato

Murray Wilson 🅜 **Professionals finalist**

Preparation time 20 minutes   **Cooking time** 1 hour   **Serves 4**

Ingredients

4 beef steak fillets, about 175g (6oz) each

1 tbsp olive oil

50g (1¾oz) unsalted butter

250g (9oz) trompette noire mushrooms, trimmed

10 sprigs of tarragon, leaves only

truffle oil, to drizzle

For the celeriac

1 large celeriac, peeled and thinly sliced

200ml (7fl oz) whole milk

200ml (7fl oz) double cream

25g (scant 1oz) unsalted butter

salt and freshly ground black pepper

For the fondant potatoes

4 large Desirée potatoes, peeled

3 tbsp duck fat

100ml (3½fl oz) chicken stock

For the jus

500ml (16fl oz) red wine

200ml (7fl oz) chicken stock

1 tbsp tomato purée

Method

1 Simmer celeriac slices in the milk and cream for 15 minutes until soft. Melt in the butter, then purée in a blender. Pass through a sieve. Season and keep warm.

2 Shape potatoes into cylinders with an apple corer. Fry in the duck fat until brown on all sides. Add stock, cover and cook for 10 minutes until soft.

3 For the jus, boil the wine until reduced by three-quarters. Add stock and reduce again by half. Stir in the tomato purée, season, and keep warm.

4 Season steaks with salt, then fry on a high heat in the oil and half the butter for 3 minutes on each side for medium-rare.

5 Sauté the mushrooms with the chopped tarragon in the remaining butter and season.

6 Arrange steaks, celeriac, potatoes and mushrooms on 4 plates. Pour over some jus.

Malaysian beef and potato curry with chapati and cucumber raita

Linda Lusardi Ⓜ **Celebrity semi-finalist**

Preparation time 45 minutes   **Cooking time** 1 hour 30 minutes   **Serves 4**

Ingredients

For the chapatis

250g (9oz) chapati or wholemeal flour, plus extra for rolling

1 tbsp vegetable oil

For the curry and rice

5 shallots, chopped

2 garlic cloves, crushed

5cm (2in) piece fresh ginger, grated

2 tbsp groundnut oil

1 tbsp hot curry powder

1 tbsp chilli powder

1 tsp ground cinnamon

1 tsp ground cumin

1 tsp ground coriander

4 curry leaves

1 star anise

4 cloves

800g (1¾lb) sirloin steak, cut into 2.5cm (1in) cubes

2 large potatoes, cut into 2.5cm (1in) cubes

2 large red chillies, deseeded and finely chopped

½tsp salt

400ml (14fl oz) coconut milk

2 tbsp lime juice

1 tsp light brown sugar

200g (7oz) basmati rice

For the cucumber raita

½ cucumber, deseeded and finely diced

200g (7oz) plain Greek yogurt

½tsp sugar

1 tbsp coriander, chopped

To garnish

2 red chillies, sliced

Method

Method

1 To make the chapatis, mix the flour with ¼ tsp salt in a large bowl. Make a well in the centre, add the oil. Gradually add 200ml (7fl oz) boiling water to form a dough. Knead on a lightly floured or oiled surface for 10 minutes, until smooth and elastic. Cover with a damp cloth and leave to rest for 45 minutes.

2 Divide the chapati dough into 8 pieces, then roll into small balls. Dust the work surface with more flour and roll out each ball into a thin disc, around 12cm (5in) in diameter.

3 Heat a non-stick frying pan over medium heat. Cook a chapati for 2 minutes on each side. Wrap and keep warm while you repeat with the remaining chapatis.

TECHNIQUE

How to knead bread dough

1 Try using a lightly oiled, rather than floured, surface for kneading. Also rub 2 tbsp of oil over dough, then fold in half, bringing the top edge towards you. It will be sticky and quite soft at this stage.

2 Use the thumb of one hand to hold the fold in place, then use the heel of your stronger hand to gently but firmly push down and away through the centre of the dough to seal the fold and stretch it.

4 Meanwhile, make the curry and rice. Fry the shallots, garlic, and ginger in the oil for 5 minutes until soft. Add all the spices and fry, stirring for 1 minute. Stir in the beef, until coated, then the potatoes, chillies, salt, and coconut milk. Bring to the boil, cover, reduce the heat, and simmer for 40 minutes, stirring occasionally. Stir in the lime juice and brown sugar, and cook uncovered for 2 minutes more. Keep hot.

5 Cook the rice according to packet directions. Drain. Keep hot.

6 Mix the raita ingredients together in a bowl. Season to taste.

7 Serve curry with the rice, raita, and chapatis, and garnished with the sliced red chillies.

3 Lift dough and rotate it a quarter turn. Repeat the folding, pushing, and rotating 10–12 times. Then place in an oiled bowl, seam-side down, cover with a cloth, and leave to prove for 10 minutes.

4 Knead dough again, as before, twice, with 10 minutes between each knead. Each time you do this it will require less oil. By the end, the dough will become noticably more elastic and even silken

Roast lamb with spinach mousse, wild garlic purée, mushrooms, and potato

Christos Georgakis ⓜ Professionals quarter-finalist

Preparation time 30 minutes   **Cooking time** 55 minutes   **Serves 4**

For the spinach mousse

400g (14oz) baby spinach

250g (9oz) cooked skinless chicken breasts, chopped

salt and freshly ground black pepper

200ml (7fl oz) double cream

50g (1¾oz) crème fraîche

For the lamb

2 fillets of lamb, about 300g (10oz) each

4 tbsp olive oil

small bunch of tarragon, chopped

small bunch of chervil, chopped

small bunch of chives, chopped

50g (1¾oz) Dijon mustard

500g (1lb 2oz) pork caul

200g (7oz) spinach leaves

60g (2oz) salted butter

For the garlic confit

12 garlic cloves

3 sprigs of thyme

3 tbsp olive oil

25g (scant 1oz) sea salt

For the potato

2 large Maris Piper potatoes, peeled

3 tbsp corn oil

150g (5½oz) salted butter

2 garlic cloves

For the balsamic jus

1 garlic clove, chopped

1 tbsp redcurrant jelly

juice of 1 lemon

4 tsp balsamic vinegar

4 sprigs of thyme

12 vine-ripened tomatoes

300ml (10fl oz) lamb stock

For the wild garlic purée

200g (7oz) wild garlic leaves

3 tbsp double cream

50g (1¾oz) unsalted butter

3 tbsp water

For the mushroom duxelle

50g (1¾oz) salted butter

3 large shallots, chopped

300g (10oz) wild mushrooms, trimmed and finely chopped

Method

1 Preheat the oven to 180°C (350°F/Gas 4). To make the spinach mousse, blanch the spinach in salted hot water for 1 minute, then refresh in cold water. Drain the leaves and leave it to dry. Put the chicken in a food processor, season with salt and pepper and blend to a purée. Add the spinach and start the food processor again. Mix together the cream and crème fraîche and pour slowly into the spinach and chicken until it combines to make a mousse. Place in a metal bowl and leave in the fridge until needed.

2 For the lamb, trim and remove excess fat from the fillets. Season with salt and pepper and, in a large frying pan, sauté in the olive oil over a high heat for 1 minute on each side. Meanwhile, mix the chopped herb leaves in a bowl with salt and pepper. Remove the fillets from the pan and wipe off the fat with kitchen paper. Brush the fillets with the Dijon mustard and cover with the herb mixture.

3 Lay out a 30cm (12in) square of pork caul and cover with half the spinach leaves. Spoon a generous amount of spinach mousse over one side of a fillet and place this side down on top of the spinach leaves on the caul. Cover the other side of the fillet with spinach mousse and then carefully wrap the caul around the fillet, tucking the ends round and under. Transfer to a roasting tin, and repeat for the second lamb fillet. Cook for 12–14 minutes in the hot oven, depending on how pink you prefer your lamb. Remove from the oven and allow lamb to rest for 10 minutes before serving. Leave the oven on.

4 Meanwhile, make the garlic confit. Put all the ingredients in a square of foil and fold to make a parcel, ensuring all edges are sealed.

Bake in the hot oven for 15–20 minutes until garlic has softened. Drain the oil and remove the thyme sprigs. Keep warm until serving.

5 For the fondant potato, cut each potato into two slabs 4cm (1½in) thick. In a saucepan, heat the oil and fry the slabs for 4–5 minutes on each side until golden brown. Add the butter, garlic cloves, seasoning, and 250ml (8fl oz) water. Bring to a simmer, cover the pan and let the potatoes cook for 15–20 minutes or until soft in the centre. Drain and keep warm.

6 To make the balsamic jus, combine all the ingredients in a small saucepan and simmer for 30 minutes. Leave to infuse in a warm place and strain before serving.

7 For the wild garlic purée, blanch the garlic leaves in boiling water for 30 seconds, remove from the water and refresh in cold water. Bring the cream, water, and butter to the boil in a saucepan. Put the garlic leaves into a blender, add the boiling liquid and blend to a smooth purée.

8 To make the mushroom duxelle, melt the butter in a frying pan, add the shallots and mushrooms and season with salt and pepper. Cook over a medium to low heat for 8–10 minutes until the vegetables are brown and the water from the mushrooms has evaporated.

9 To assemble, slice the lamb and arrange 3–4 thick slices on a bed of mushrooms on each of 4 serving plates. Serve the potato fondant alongside, together with a pool of wild garlic purée and some of the garlic confit. Pour over the jus and serve immediately.

Index

Acknowledgments

Shine TV and Endemol Shine Group would like to thank:
Frances Adams, David Ambler, Alice Bernardi, Martin Buckett, Claire Burton, Bev Comboy, Kerisa Edwards, Jessica Hannan, Ozen Kazim, Angela Loftus, Lou Plank, Lyndsey Posner, Franc Roddam, John Torode, and Gregg Wallace.

MasterChef alumni whose recipes and quotes are reproduced in this book:
Tim Anderson, Cheryl Avery, Dhruv Baker, Caroline Brewester, John Calton, Darren Campbell MBE, Alix Carwood, Nargis Chaudhary, Alice Churchill, David Coulson, Sara Danesin Medio, Matthew Driver, Lisa Faulkner, Mat Follas, Chris Gates, Christos Georgakis, David Hall, Christine Hamilton, Matt James, Jackie Kearney, Claire Lara, Kennedy Leitch, Linda Lusardi, Liz McClarnon, Perveen Nekoo, Andy Oliver, Michael Pajak, Andi Peters, Michelle Peters, Nick Pickard, Alex Rushmer, Simon Small, Christopher Souto, Neil Stuke, John Torode, Steven Wallis, Sarah Whittle, and Murray Wilson.

Dorling Kindersley would like to thank:
Libby Brown and Amy Slack for editorial assistance, Philippa Nash for design assistance, and Vanessa Bird for indexing.

Senior Editor Cécile Landau
Senior Art Editor Alison Shackleton
Managing Editor Stephanie Farrow
Managing Art Editor Christine Keilty
Jacket Designer Steven Marsden
Producer, Pre-Production Robert Dunn
Producer Stephanie McConnell
Special Sales Creative Project Manager
Alison Donovan
Art Director Maxine Pedliham
Publisher Mary-Clare Jerram

First published in Great Britain in 2018 by
Dorling Kindersley Limited, 80 Strand, London, WC2R 0RL
A Penguin Random House Company

Material previous published in:
The MasterChef Cookbook (2010), MasterChef At Home (2011),
MasterChef Kitchen Bible (2011),
and MasterChef Everyday (2012)

10 9 8 7 6 5 4 3 2 1
001—309621—Feb/2018

A CIP catalogue record for this book is available
from the British Library.
ISBN 978-0-2413-3338-9

MasterChef
www.masterchef.com

A WORLD OF IDEAS:
SEE ALL THERE IS TO KNOW
www.dk.com